MW01226259

The Rune Book

by

Woden's Folk Kindred

The Rune Book © 2020 by Woden's Folk Kindred. All rights reserved. No part of this book may be used or reproduced in any manner whatsoever, including Internet usage, without written permission from Woden's Folk Kindred, except in the case of brief quotations embodied in critical articles and reviews.

First Edition
ISBN 9798654294999
Book design by Berk Harbin
Cover art © 2020
Edited by Woden's Folk Kindred and Karen M.P. Carlson
Illustrations by Berk Harbin and Dawn Thomas

Woden's Folk Kindred is a 501(c)3 nonprofit church incorporated in the State of Texas. All profits associated with this book go towards funding Woden's Folk Kindred and its programs.

Woden's Folk Kindred
302 Dewberry St.
Waxahachie, TX 75165

wodensfolkkindred.org

Visit our page, Woden's Folk Kindred, on Facebook or Instagram

Other titles available
on Amazon by
Woden's Folk Kindred:

FOREWORD

This book has been a long time in the publishing, but the manuscript has been written for years. It has been pushed off and pushed away for other projects, notably our work on the Heilvegr. This was probably a good thing, because the Heilvegr Fellowship has really taken off, and it is helping a lot of people to get their lives back on a better path, but we finally got this book published, so that those who need a better grasp of the runes can have that understanding.

The Rune Book is chiefly the work of Jayson Hawkins with a good deal of input from Thorstein Mayfield. Jim Hawkins, Jim Flournoy, and Valin Klock did a great job preparing the maunuscript. Special thanks must also be given again to our wonderful editor, Karen MP Carlson. She makes things so easy for us, and knowing that she's on our team makes things a lot less stressful. Thank you, Karen.

The artwork for this book is the result of a collaboration between Dawn Thomas and myself. We worked hard trying to find a good balance between the roughness of our sketches and the exacting images we grafted onto them with Photoshop. The idea was for the illustrations to be like the runes themselves in that they are frameworks that contain certain elements. Each one, like each rune, should provide a small framework to help understand the subject rune.

A final thanks also goes out to Dawn Thomas. During the work on this book, in a purely wyrd way, she was looking through one of her old dicitonaries and asked if I knew that elk was an old word for a goose or swan. This led us down the road to a greater understanding of the Algiz rune, and I think many people will benefit in their understanding of the runes from that small bit of lore that was found in a forgotten old tome.

    I am certain that there are still mistakes to be found in this book, and I will take all of the credit for those. I am equally certain, however, that the great information to be found in this book far outweighs the few faults. It gives me great pride and joy to be able to be a part of producing this work, and I hope that you enjoy *The Rune Book*.

By the Gods,
Berk

Abbreviations

AS	Anglo-Saxon
OE	Old English
OHG	Old High German
OI	Old Icelandic
ON	Old Norse
PIE	Proto-Indo-European

INTRODUCTION

The runes are without question the most fascinating relics of the great legacy of Heathen Europe. Ancient inscriptions offer silent testimony that the world of the North was once a very different place, and they present almost irresistible clues that draw the curious into the greater riddle that seeks who our ancestors were and what they believed.

Even popular culture is not immune to runic charm. From the creations of J.R.R. Tolkien and J.K. Rowling to the album cover of Led Zeppelin Four, we constantly encounter evidence of how the runes continue to enchant the descendants of the people who created them.

Runes have a special significance for modern Heathens as we strive to firmly reconnect with the ways of our ancestors. The runes give us a glimpse of the worldview of the ancient North, and they present the possibility of unlocking some of the many puzzles that confront us in our ancestral mythology, culture, and ritual.

Heathens generally agree on very little, but nearly all of us agree on the importance of the runes in our way. The problems start when we move beyond that basic agreement and talk about what the runes mean to us and how best to learn about them, which brings us to the purpose of this book.

Every author has an agenda, a reason behind their writing. We are no exception. On numerous occasions over the years we have been asked to recommend a book to someone who was curious about the runes, but we have never been able to do so without reservations. Although there are a few excellent rune books on the market, no one text addresses all the relevant issues and none approach the subject from a purely Heathen perspective. When it became apparent that this ideal rune book did not exist, we set out to create it. By combining the best scholarship in the field with our own research into the beliefs and practices of our Northern European ancestors, we hope to have achieved our goal.

In each section of this book, we try to approach our subject from two directions. Archaeology and ancient literature provide the base from which we examine our topics using modern ideas about psychology, mythology, history, and philosophy. At the same time, we are Heathen, so we explain how the runes are a living force in our lives. We hope that this dual approach provides readers with both the information they need to build a working understanding of the runic tradition and a starting point from which they can successfully begin to make the runes an important part of their own lives.

RUNE BOOKS

Before delving into the runes themselves, it may be useful to get a sense of the kinds of information available on the subject. In the course of our research over the past decade, we observed that rune books fall into two basic categories. Each presents specific advantages and disadvantages to those who are new to the topic, and we believe our readers will benefit from an investigation into the differing viewpoints from which these texts are written as well as their strengths and weaknesses.

Historical Texts

The first category we will call the historical. These texts are usually written by university professors for a largely academic audience. The information they present focuses on archaeological evidence, and conclusions are drawn based on the author's interpretation of history. These books can be very helpful, as they place the runes in the cultural context in which they originated. In other words, they offer us insight into how our ancestors used and understood the staves and can teach us much about our heritage.

There are, however, a few disadvantages to historical texts. One is that they are usually intended for readers who have college backgrounds in related fields. As such, they assume a core of knowledge that a person new to the runes may lack. Some of the information presented may seem "over one's head" and leave neophytes feeling that runic studies are best left to students willing to major in ancient Germanic languages. With a bit of dedication and perseverance this obstacle can be overcome, though; after familiarizing themselves with the terminology, the readers will find these books less daunting than they first appeared.

The bigger problem with historical texts is that they treat the runes as an antiquity — a system whose usefulness died along with the Viking Age. In this view, the runes have limited appeal or practical value beyond the halls of academia. The authors of these books, whether they call themselves Christian or not, operate from the Judeo-Christian worldview of our contemporary society which considers the coming of the desert faith to Northern Europe to be the absolute end of pagan practices for the peoples of that region. For the Heathens of today, this simply is not true. The runes form a vital part of a living tradition that links us back to the old ways. While we do not make the untenable claim that the chain of tradition between us and our forebears remained unbroken despite a thousand years of suppression by a foreign creed, we do believe that the study of the runes can help bridge the gap and reconnect us to our heritage.

The runes have always been more than engravings on ancient stones; they are a means to a deeper relationship with our people, ourselves, and the world around us. Despite these limitations, most historical texts will prove invaluable to the serious runester. The works of R.I. Page are readily available and provide an excellent source of information.

One caveat with Page, however, is his odd insistence that the runes were never used for magical purposes. He seems unfamiliar with the Eddas and sagas, which depict both gods and men employing runes to achieve magical ends, but even if we look only at archaeological evidence there are numerous artifacts that attest to the runes being intimately bound to magic.

A more balanced approach is taken by Ralph Elliott, who contends that some runic inscriptions are obviously magical in nature while others are open to debate. His *Runes: An Introduction* is highly recommended to readers who want to further their knowledge.

Pop-Occult Books

The other common category of rune books is what we will refer to as pop-occult. These texts are written by anyone who feels they have the authority to do so and are aimed at a wider audience, particularly readers curious about "secret" knowledge. The information they present refers to historical facts only when convenient to the author; otherwise, it comes from a hodge-podge of New Age ideas or the writer's own imagination. These books are not without value though. To their credit, they present the runes as a living system with applications viable in this day and age. They encourage the reader to experience the runes on a personal level and integrate the concepts they embody into their lives. These books also expose many folks to the runes who may not have encountered them otherwise and offer a convenient introduction to the staves.

Before going any further, we need to define what we mean by the terms "occult" and "pop-occult." For our purposes, an occult text is one that imparts information that is "secret" or known only to an initiated few. In academic lingo, an occult text would be considered a primary source, whereas a pop-occult book is a secondary source — a commentary that attempts to explain, compare, or combine primary sources. Occult texts tend to be quite old, typically dating back to medieval times (although a few are much more ancient), whereas pop-occult books came into fashion in the late nineteenth century and became widely popular in the second half of the twentieth.

Occult ideas pose problems when they are applied to the runes or to Heathenry in general, and these problems are both serious and common enough that they need to be addressed here. The occult "doctrine of correspondences" — which supposes that any aspect of one system can be matched or correlated to a particular aspect of any other system — arises from the idea that all the world's knowledge originates in Atlantis (or Lemuria, Thule, etc.). The story goes that when this mysterious land was destroyed by a cataclysmic disaster, the keepers of its knowledge escaped to the four corners of the earth and began instructing new initiates to pass on their wisdom. Thus wherever occult traditions are found, they are merely different expressions of the "Atlantian" corpus, and correspondences can be found that equate one with any other. The twenty-two Major Arcana of the Tarot can thus be matched to the twenty-two letters of the Hebrew alphabet and the twenty-two pathways joining the ten sephiroth of the Kabalistic Tree of Life. Less obvious are how these twenty-two concepts pair up with the dozen signs of the zodiac, the seven ancient planets, the eight (formerly nine) modern planets, the sixty-four I Ching hexagrams, the four elements (earth, air, fire, water), the various alchemical stages/metals, and innumerable aspects of other systems. It is the task of pop-occult authors to decipher these "hidden" correspondences and unravel them for their audience; however, scrutiny of their methods reveals that their claims rest on no verifiable authority outside of the writer's own intuition.

Even in cases where the number of aspects of one system sync up with those of another, it is either happy accident (as with the Tarot cards and the Hebrew letters) or because the more recent system was designed to match an older one (as the pathways on the Tree of Life are specifically drawn to accommodate the number of Hebrew letters). Either way, the particular pairing of one aspect with any other is arbitrary and limited only by the creative imagination of the author.

The hole in the Atlantis theory and its doctrine of correspondences, aside from the total absence of material evidence, is that people are not everywhere the same. Different systems developed independently of one another to meet the needs of different peoples as they interacted with diverse environments.

Tribes in equatorial desert regions encounter vastly different challenges than those in the icy mountains of the North, and these differences shape the mental maps of the respective peoples — from language to skill set to mythology. Although history demonstrates a borrowing of ideas and technology between peoples in war and trade, as we will discuss later, to posit the existence of a world-wide monoculture as their point of origin requires a willful ignorance of the facts.

Few folks today believe in an actual sunken continent, but the notions embodied by Atlantis live on in the modern umbrella of "universalism." This stance holds that all peoples are inherently the same, and all the world's traditions belong equally to all peoples. There is thus no reason why it would be inappropriate or paradoxical for an individual of one culture to adopt the practices of any other. As adherents of this view are wont to say, "There are many paths up the mountain, but they all lead to the top."

In contrast to this, resurgent ancestral faiths such as Heathenry embrace "folkishness" — the position that our differences are not only real but should be celebrated. Folkishness promotes true diversity by recognizing the unique contributions of different peoples, and it is precisely these differences that define our culture, heritage, and identity. To phrase it another way, there are not only many paths but many different mountains.

Rune studies have proven especially attractive to occult writers, and the problems associated with occult doctrine often crop up in popular rune books. One reason for this problem is that when studying the runes, primary sources are almost always inscriptions on ancient artifacts, weapons, tree bark, memorial stones, etc. — rather than actual manuscripts. These are occult in the sense that few people today can translate them, and even fewer (if any) are able to grasp the full meaning or intention of the carver. In the majority of cases, we can at best hazard an educated guess. It is doubtful that many folks could read and interpret these inscriptions even at the time they were produced.

The scarcity of solid information invites speculation, which should be encouraged when centered in the appropriate historical and geographic context. In other words, trying to apply the tactics of the French Foreign Legion, African Zulu warriors, or Japanese Samurai to the nearly three thousand year old text of the *Iliad* may deepen our appreciation for Homer's epic, but it will not bring us any closer to understanding the poet's words. Only by examining other works and archaeological finds from his place and time can we hope to shed light on obscure passages.

The same holds true for the runes. Unfortunately, pop-occult authors of the early twentieth century Germanic Renaissance were heavily influenced by Theosophy and its fascination with Hindu mysticism. Authors such as Friedrich Bernhard Marby, Siegfried Adolf Kummer, and Karl Maria Wiligut put a runic gloss on Eastern practices like yoga and chanting (mantras). Guido von List went so far as to reject the ancient futharks entirely and invent another one that suited his own theories. While these new systems demonstrated the ingenuity of their creators, they had no real tie to the actual runes or any other part of our heritage.

The current crop of pop-occult books often suffer from the same flaw. Unlike historical texts, they generally lack anything deeper than a superficial connection to our ancestral culture. Several suggest that runes served as a sort of magical alphabet for a hypothetical Viking priesthood, but beyond such misleading claims they leave the reader with the impression that the futhark belongs to a global network of secret initiates.

These books tend to present the runes as interchangeable with the Tarot, I Ching, Kabbala, or other occult systems and include lists of colors, gemstones, animals, trees, deities, astrological signs, etc. that correspond to each stave. While a few runes do represent animals (Fehu, Uruz, Ehwaz, and possibly Algiz), trees (Eihwaz and Berkano), and gods (Ansuz, Tiwaz, and Inguz), attempts to relate every stave to all the categories above have no basis in fact or in tradition. A book that claims, for example, "Thurisaz is the rune of butterflies and baboons, its color is dark green, and its stone is topaz," is purely the invention of the author. These correspondences may entertain some readers, but they have no value for Heathens or anyone wishing to understand the runes in their context. As a result, many pop-occult books are near useless.

Other Authors

Before moving on, a few words should be said regarding two of the more popular contemporary writers. About thirty years ago a pair of the earliest pop-occult books about the runes appeared on the market — Ralph Blum's *The Book of Runes* and Edred Thorsson's *Futhark*. For better or worse, these texts set the benchmark for the dozens of authors who have followed in their wake. Despite both having a long-lasting impact, these books take a very different approach to the runes, and it is best if we examine them separately.

First published in 1982, Blum's *The Book of Runes* has exposed thousands of readers to the staves of the Elder Futhark; unfortunately, it is also the source of several unfounded ideas still seen in rune texts today. Among these are many of his "meanings" for individual staves that bear no relation to the actual rune-names. Subsequent pop-occult authors seem to have adopted this stance as a license to ignore tradition and attach any meaning to a rune they see fit. Another of Blum's wilder notions is his random rearrangement of the futhark order. Although no contemporary authors have repeated this blunder to our knowledge, it does demonstrate an absence of respect for our heritage. Yet the one concept of Blum's that has drawn the most ire from his critics is the introduction of a twenty-fifth stave — the so-called "blank rune" which Dr. Stephen Flowers calls "inauthentic and extremely counter-productive."

For all these reasons, Ralph Elliott includes Blum's *The Book of Runes* as part of a "steady flow of dubious publications designed for a credulous and superstitious public." Finally, Kveldulf Gundarsson, another erudite scholar of Germanic languages, recommends bluntly that if you own any of Blum's work, "throw it away. " To his credit, Blum readily admits he had little experience with the runes prior to writing the book and was thus ignorant of the 2,000 years of tradition he had tossed out the window; sadly, this is no compensation to those who have purchased his books and trusted him as an authority on the subject.

Coming on the heels of *The Book of Runes*, Edred Thorsson's *Futhark* appeared on bookshelves in 1984. Unlike its predecessor, *Futhark* approached the runes from a traditional standpoint, keeping the original order of the staves and building on the actual meanings of the rune names. As such, this book has long been considered the classic of the genre by Heathens and others who value Germanic heritage. It is not without its faults, though. While *Futhark* is grounded in ancestral tradition, it also incorporates elements of foreign occult systems. The same could be said of other early Thorsson works, especially *Nine Doors of Midgard*. This marked influence in Thorsson's writing can be traced to an obsession with the esoteric arts in his youth. In the early-mid '70s, he describes himself as a "hopeless occultnik," and it was in the midst of this period that he heard a voice in his head speak the word *"runa"* —

an event that would impact the course of his life from then on. We have no reason to doubt the veracity of this UPG (unverifiable personal gnosis), but the reason we mention it is to point out his gateway into runic studies opened during a time when he was immersed in the occult. As this was his "point of contact" with folkish tradition, it perhaps makes sense that his initial works were tinted through a lens of alien occultism.

It should be mentioned that Thorsson, whose given name is Stephen Edred Flowers, earned a Ph.D. from the University of Texas with a dissertation entitled *Runes and Magic*. He also studied for years in Germany at the University of Göttingen. Few, if any, other pop-occult writers can match his credentials, but in recent years his literary output has tended more toward historical texts about Northern European peoples, traditions, and languages. These later works, published under the name Dr. Stephen E. Flowers, are accessible to the average reader and come recommended to those who wish to widen their knowledge of Heathen history and heritage. His pop-occult hooks, which usually appear under the nom de plume Edred Thorsson, could be considered the best of a questionable genre. While they contain much useful information, they also host many concepts that fall outside of our ancestral traditions. Experienced students should have little trouble weeding out these foreign elements, but newer readers would be well-advised to approach the Thorsson titles with a grain of salt rather than swallow them whole.

Conclusions

It should be said at this point that the above is not a condemnation of pop-occult books on runes or any other subject. It is just important to understand that such books are not Heathen because they are not concerned with tradition or culture.

In creating this book, we try to take everything our source material offers us, and then use our unique Heathen perspective to piece the puzzle together in ways that often do not occur to others, including scholars, occult writers, or other pagans. We do not hesitate to offer our own speculations, but we separate speculation from fact. More importantly, our speculations are based on evidence from our culture and are intended as practical guides for Heathens.

ORIGIN AND HISTORY OF THE FUTHARK

What is a Rune?

Any attempt to understand runes or their origins must begin with a firm idea of exactly what a rune is. Dictionaries define a rune as a letter of the earliest German script, but the practice of defining runes solely as a system of writing is modern and incomplete. Older meanings of the word rune point towards broader concepts.

Rune can mean "secret, mystery, or whisper" in the elder Germanic languages. The Gothic *Bible* translates "the mystery of the kingdom of God" as "*runa thiud angjard os guds*," and the Old English poem *The Wanderer* calls the solitary contemplation of a wise man his "*run*." (Elliott, 1) In Old Norse, "*eyraruna*" is a woman in an especially intimate relationship with a man, perhaps referring to the secrets they share (*eyra*=ear, *runa*= secret or whisper). When "rune" passed from Germanic languages to the tongues of neighboring peoples, it carried the broader meaning. "*Run*" means "secret" in Old Irish and Scotch Gaelic, and "*urhin*" carries the same meaning in Welsh. The Finnish word "*runo*" means "song," which in a Heathen context could easily carry meanings of "spell" or "charm."

No source in the lore speaks more about runes than *Havamal*, and Odin's words convey a broad meaning of the term rune. He says he was silent and thoughtful at the Well of Urd: "I listened to the speech of men,/ of runes I heard them speak,/ nor were they silent in counsel." (st. 111) While this passage points toward a meaning of secret or mystery, Odin later speaks of "counseling staves, very potent staves, very strong staves,/ that the mighty sage drew, and the great gods made,/ and Hropt (Odin) carved with power." (st. 142) This passage is obviously referring to a script, called staves or runestaves, yet it also seems the staves themselves inherently possess power or perhaps can convey the power of the secret or mystery they represent. There is no easy definition for rune. The entire system of meaning carried by the word is perhaps mirrored in the complex meanings of each individual rune, but it is clear that by limiting our definition, we risk missing the enormous scope of knowledge the runes convey. To better understand the full concept of runes, we will examine their origins, both as staves and mysteries, and their evolution as a system.

ORIGINS OF THE ELDER FUTHARK

Runes

I know that I hung
upon a tree, exposed to the wind,
nights all nine, wounded by spear
and given to Odin, myself to myself,

13

on that tree which no man knows
from whence that root runs.
Not with loaf or with horn did they bless me,
I peered down, I took up the runes,
crying out, I took them,
then I fell back from there.

Havamal, 138-139

The stark vision of Odin in the grip of transformational ecstasy upon the World Tree is an iconic image both in Odin's cult and Heathenry in general. The grasping of the runes is a pivotal moment in the mythology of the North. Odin is forever changed, and he in turn changes the cosmos and initiates the chain of events that leads to the creation of Midgard.

Subsequent stanzas paint an awe-inspiring picture of Odin's new-found skills, and though staves are mentioned, the list of magical feats goes far beyond literacy. This conclusion leads us to ask just what Odin took into his hands when he grasped the runes, and the answer goes to the core of Odinic myth. Odin's appearance on the mythic stage marks a dramatic shift in the landscape. This shift is rooted in consciousness, and it gives Odin a tremendous advantage. Odin is capable of recognizing the cosmos as a functioning entity, and he recognizes his own identity as separate from his environment and yet integrated into it. This allows him to examine the cosmos and its immutable laws; examine his own characteristics, capabilities, and limitations; and understand how he can affect the cosmos and be affected by it. For the first time, there is a consciousness capable of truly seeing its environment, envisioning a fundamentally different world, and then acting to make that vision a reality. Prior to this moment, mythic figures were carried by events. Odin is now equipped to set his own agenda.

With this new ability, Odin continues to gather knowledge of the cosmos. He learns "nine mighty songs" from "the son of Bolthorn" who is probably Mimir. He gets a drink of the magical mead Odroerir. These secrets and mysteries can also be considered runes, and Odin goes beyond just learning from others — *Havamal* says he carved some himself.

Judging from the skills listed in *Havamal*, and similar skill sets listed in *Grogaldr*, *Sigrdrifumal*, and *Rigsthula*, the runelore Odin learned included magical spells that could control the weather, heal the sick, protect his friends in battle, or win a maiden's love. These skills would appear to point back to the idea mentioned earlier, that of Odin being able to understand his world and affect it. Even if the magical element is eliminated, the idea of a body of systematized knowledge and a cognitive or philosophical method for putting that knowledge to use remains. The existence of this system is probably being referred to when Odin talks of healing skills (*Hav.* 146-147) and a knowledge of history and myth (*Hav.* 159). Looking deeper at a few other stanzas reveals strategic thinking in war (*Hav.* 156), the ability to mitigate social conflict (*Hav.* 150, 153, and probably 152), and a working knowledge of the weather (*Hav.* 154). The line between magic and knowledge is blurry, thus the idea of mystery and secret.

Coupled with the prosaic skill above are the skills of the shaman. There is absolutely no doubt that the shamanic art was practiced in the North, nor is there any doubt that this art was part of Odin's cult. The secrets of the shaman include projecting the spirit out of the body to both observe and affect the unseen forces that influence the lives of men. These secrets were also systematized and included knowledge of medicine, the natural world, and astronomy. These runes were part of the knowledge Odin won, and much of it came into the hands of men.

In this sense, a rune could be a piece of knowledge, a skill, or even the methods used to learn or remember. It is a well-documented fact that our ancestors, like other preliterate societies, possessed encyclopaedic knowledge of their world. This knowledge was all passed down orally and committed to memory. Celtic druids were said to spend twenty years in learning, and the transmission of such ancestral knowledge is probably being referred to in *Rigsthula* when Rig teaches runes to his son Jarl, who in turn passes them on to his son Kon (st. 37, 44-46). This collected knowledge, the techniques that grew from it, and the system used to transmit and remember it, could all be seen as runes.

We do not know for certain what the system looked like or how it worked in the earliest times. It is interesting to speculate about the relationship the entire body of knowledge had with the futhark. Perhaps a system was conceived that centered on language. The futhark contains all the sounds of the elder Germanic language, and it could therefore be thought of as capable of describing everything in our ancestors' world. The rune-names and phonetic values associated with them might therefore predate the staves by a considerable period. This could help explain the unique order of the futhark and the inclusion of so many indigenous symbols in the stave system.

Staves

The problem of the origin of the twenty-four stave system of the Elder Futhark has mystified generations of scholars. Unfortunately, many of the efforts to solve the problem have been influenced by a drive to prove a point about Germanic culture in the Iron Age. Some nationalist scholars have put forward theories for a purely Germanic origin of the runes as part of larger attempts to trace all cultural advances back to an idealized proto-Aryan civilization in Northern Europe.

At the other end of the spectrum, a large number of scholars have theorized that the Germans adapted the runic script straight from one of their literate neighbors, because after all, hairy Heathen barbarians could not have created anything sophisticated on their own. Both these theories are skewed by pre-conceived notions about the Germans, and both theories studiously ignore any contradictory evidence. The truth, as is usually the case, lies somewhere in the middle.

There is evidence from late Neolithic and Bronze Age carvings in Scandinavia of the use of symbols in ritual settings. Eleven of these symbols are found in the Elder Futhark, but there is no evidence that these symbols were used for writing as we know it before the creation of the futhark. In other words, the symbol X was used on rock carvings, but there is no way for us to tell if it meant "gebo/gift," and there is certainly no evidence it phonetically represented the letter G.

The remaining staves of the futhark appear to be derived from the alphabetic scripts of Mediterranean civilizations, though which of these civilizations provided the model is debated among scholars. To understand how this derivation took place, it is important to understand the nature of the contact that existed between the Germans and their neighbors to the south. This contact took two primary forms: trade and war.

The Alps and the Black Forest were daunting barriers that effectively separated Mediterranean Europe from

Northern Europe for centuries, but no barrier has ever proven impassable where intrepid traders smell profit. Amber and walrus ivory provided the ultimate lure for merchants — they are both easily portable, plentiful and cheap at their source, yet rare and expensive in their final markets. Northern Italy was an emporium for these products, and the route down from the Baltic, across the Alps, and on to the Adriatic Sea was regularly traveled from the Bronze Age up through Classical times. Traders from the North exchanged their amber, ivory, and later furs for finely worked prestige items — gold, jewels, and ornamented weapons.

This type of trade involved a depth of cultural and personal contact that is difficult for modern people to fully grasp. There was no Walmart-style clearing house where trading was done impersonally and quickly. Traders moving across the Alps were limited to one or at most two trips per year. They would have spent long periods in the lands of their trading partners. They would need to learn the language and gain a working knowledge of the culture. If later patterns of trade are any guide, there may have been permanent trading settlements in both Germany and Italy.

A Germanic trader in Italy at any time from 500 BCE onward would have been exposed to Latin, Greek, and Etruscan culture. Merchants that plied the Adriatic in this era had to be fluent and literate in several languages, and because literacy has everywhere been the child of commerce, it is quite likely that the first literate Germans learned to write in the language of one of their trading partners. It is only a small step from writing in a foreign language to applying this script to one's native tongue. The Negau helmet, which appears to contain a Germanic inscription in a North Italic alphabet, is evidence the Germans took this step.

The second main point of contact between the Germans and their southern neighbors was war. Robbery and brigandage are the constant companions of trade, but real war required the movement of large numbers of men across the barriers mentioned above. The Germans' Celtic neighbors crossed those barriers in search of land and plunder in 400 BCE, but the Germans would wait nearly three hundred years before venturing south in force.

The Germans made their military debut in Italy in 110 BCE with the tribal invasion of the Cimbri and Teutones. These tribes would wander, fight, and pillage their way across Northern Italy and Southern Gaul for ten years. They sacked cities, took innumerable prisoners, and swelled their ranks by accepting Italian outlaws and runaway slaves before being crushed by Gaius Marius in two battles in 100 BCE. These Germans were believed to have come from the far north, so they were not nearly as familiar with Italy as the Alpine tribes, but by the end of their campaign they had been exposed to every facet of Italian life. Many tribesmen escaped after their defeat, but many thousands were taken as slaves. A significant number of these would have eventually made the journey home as well. The threat of the Germans faded for a time, but Julius Caesar, who was born in the year of Marius' triumphs, had to rush north to face an invasion of Suebi. After defeating them, Caesar incorporated large numbers of Germans into his army. No Roman army of note would ever march again without a German contingent. The barriers that had separated the Germans from the south were permanently overcome, and in their place was a frontier several hundred miles long.

Germans were now an ever-present part of Roman life, and Mediterranean culture began to exert increasing influence on the Germanic tribes. A cultural point where trade and war met with saddening frequency in the ancient world was slavery. Tens of thousands of Germans were enslaved after being defeated by the Romans, and there was probably a steady flow of Italians slaves into the North as war booty and skilled labor.

The likely result of all this contact was a number of people with substantial knowledge of both cultures: Etruscan or Roman traders who spent years in Germany, Cimbri who looted in Italy as invaders and then labored there as slaves after defeat, German mercenaries who spent decades in the legions before returning home, or runaway Italian slaves who joined German raiders and followed their new companions back north. The point is that the scripts of the Classical world were transmitted to the North through a variety of means, and even though literacy in any language was certainly rare among the Germans in the first millennium of our era, it was not completely unknown. The tools for adapting southern scripts to the Germanic languages were available, and enough people had been sufficiently exposed to civilization to understand the value of such an adaptation.

It is therefore quite remarkable that when the futhark was created, it was not the type of adaption usually seen in the ancient world. The Roman alphabet, for example, was adapted from the Greeks, who in turn got it from the Phoenicians. This adaptation included not just shapes but the order, letter names, and sound values. In the futhark, on the other hand, only thirteen of the twenty-four staves are clearly from foreign scripts. They were taken mostly from Northern Italic sources, but also from Latin and Greek. The alpha-beta order is abandoned completely, the stave names are clearly Germanic in origin, and more often than not, adapted shapes carry different phonetic values in the futhark. Considering these facts, it would perhaps be better to think of the futhark as a native Germanic creation that was substantially influenced by the scripts of the Mediterranean world, but even this conditional conclusion is subject to debate, and many questions remain unanswered.

The most intriguing of these questions are how the futhark was created and why it was done at all. Understanding how the futhark was created revolves around how the shapes were chosen for each stave. It is probably a fairly safe assumption that whoever put the futhark together was literate in one or more of the languages of the south, otherwise there would be even less influence from these scripts. Yet, as mentioned above, our inventor did not adapt one of these systems straight into the Germanic language.

We can safely conclude this not only for the reasons already discussed, but also because we have another example of a Germanic language being written in an alphabet heavily influenced by an existing script. The Gothic *Bible* was translated into Gothic from Greek by Ulfilas in the fourth century CE. He created a Gothic script by drawing heavily on Greek and Latin forms, even though the futhark was known to him. Ulfilas uses only two obvious runic forms; the majority of the rest are Greek or Latin. Considering that the creator of the futhark had no stave tradition to work from, the fact that the futhark uses more indigenous symbols than the Gothic script shows that this creator was making every effort to tie the futhark to Germanic forms and traditions.

The shapes of the staves were also influenced by other factors.

The first of these was how the staves were carved. The oldest existing inscriptions are on stone and metal, but it is almost certain that wood was the most common surface for rune carving. Staves were carved across the grain. This is why there are no horizontal lines in the staves, because such lines would split the wood along the grain. The problems of carving on wood also influenced the shapes of the staves because there are only so many convenient shapes to carve within the limitations of the available tools.

Other scripts shared these limitations in their early history, but because of the widespread use of ink for writing in the civilized world, letter forms had become more fluid and varied. We are left to conclude that the inventor of the futhark chose the shapes of the staves both because he wished the system to have Germanic roots and because any adapted staves would have to be easy to carve across wood grain.

This leaves the question of why the futhark was created at all. To fully answer this question we must put aside modern assumptions about the inherent value, even necessity, of literacy. Such assumptions were not part of the Heathen culture of the North two thousand years ago and the Germans had not reached a point in their social development that not being able to write was holding them back. Even if literacy was the goal, the creation of the futhark was unnecessary. The druids were literate in Latin and Greek, so they could transmit any information they wished in those languages. The Celts did not therefore develop their own competing script. (Celtic Ogham never moved beyond epigraphs and into true writing.) Yet even though there were certainly Germans who could read and write southern languages, they still developed the futhark.

There is no historical record of who developed the futhark or why they did so, but by looking at everything we know about runic origins, we can make some educated guesses. Whoever put the stave system together was probably trained in the system of rune knowledge discussed above. The unique order of the futhark and the elegance of the system as a whole point toward a mind well-trained in organizing information and well-informed about the nuances of Germanic mythology. He or she would also have been literate in another language, and more importantly, would have had to be intimate enough with one of the southern cultures to truly grasp the power of literacy as a tool.

A German whose only contact with literacy was watching merchants scribble sums would not have felt compelled to create the futhark; however, if that same man had stood inside a library and truly understood what he was seeing, he would have been awed by the power and potential of the written word. This awe would have been more acute in someone trained in the existing runic tradition. Yet such a man would also have understood the importance of being true to his blood and culture. The runic tradition was centuries in the making and came from the gods themselves. There could be no warping of Germanic culture to fit civilized techniques; the tools of the south would have to be bent to fit the runes.

Judging from the results, our inventor took symbols already used by his people and attached names and phonetic values for about half the futhark, then he filled in the remaining staves by using shapes from Northern Italic, Greek, and Latin scripts. Some of the phonetic values for these adapted staves are different from what they had in their original script. This is probably because in many cases the sound value the letter held in its native script was already assigned to another stave.

We can speculate endlessly about whether there was one creator or several, whether the process was drawn out or quick, and which tribe our hypothetical creator belonged to, but what is inarguable is that when the process was over, the older system of runes was tied to a new creation.

23

THE FUTHARK

This creation was the twenty-four stave system of the Elder Futhark. Though there are arguments about inscriptions that appear to be in runes in the second or third century BCE, the first time the complete futhark appears is on the early fifth century Kylver Stone from Gotland, Sweden. The date of the creation of the futhark must, of course, be older than this. The inclusion of Etruscan letter forms presupposes an origin in the days before Latin eclipsed its rivals in Italy, and this would push the creation of the futhark back to the first century CE, if not earlier.

The Etruscan connection is perhaps also important for more than shapes. A bundle of twenty sticks inscribed with Etruscan letters and numbers was discovered in the Tyrol region of Northern Italy. (Elliott, 10) These sticks were likely used for sortilege divination which could be the Italian counterpart of the Germanic divination process described by Tacitus. The creation of the futhark may have also marked a substantial modification of the favored Germanic divination system. There were local variations of the shapes, and in a few inscriptions, some variations in order. There is, however, remarkable consistency from Denmark to the shores of the Black Sea over a period of several centuries.

As mentioned previously, the order of the staves in the futhark is unique and remarkable. True alphabets are so called from the order of the first two letters — alpha and beta in Greek. The futhark takes its name from the first six staves — Fehu, Uruz, Thurisaz, Ansuz, Raidho, and Kennaz. This beginning order, and the bulk of the remaining order, is retained in its essentials throughout the subsequent evolution of the futhark. Because the futhark order is so dramatically different from that of alphabetic scripts, and because it is a constant in runic history, it seems logical to conclude that it either somehow predates the stave system or was considered so critical to the stave system that it was retained.

In addition to the order, another constant is the breaking of the twenty-four staves into three groups of eight called "aetts," a word that can mean "eight" but can also mean "family, clan, or generation." Each aett is named after the phonetic value of its first rune, rendering Frey's aett, Hagal's aett, and Tyr's aett. This system also survived subsequent changes in the number of staves in the futhark, even though later aetts often did not have eight staves.

Linguistic shifts would begin to work significant changes in the futhark among the people who continued using runes as the centuries progressed. Among the Anglo-Saxons who settled in Britain, these changes would add four runes by the seventh century, and in some versions of the Anglo-Saxon futhark, the total of staves would reach thirty-three. These changes mirrored those in language and were also part of the secularization of the runes after conversion.

In Scandinavia, significant linguistic changes had the opposite effect. As sounds disappeared and emerged in the spoken language, the Scandinavians opted to let existing staves stand for multiple sounds rather than add new shapes. The eventual result was a shrinking of the futhark to sixteen staves throughout Scandinavia by the ninth century. This shorter system is called the Younger Futhark.

It is difficult to speculate on what these changes meant for how the futhark fit into the larger body of runelore described above. It may be that changes in this elder system, or the evolution of the stave system, may mark the first stirrings of a shift away from traditional culture toward the civilization of the south. One thing to remember is that the Elder Futhark was still in use in many of the lands where the changes took place, and archaic rune forms continue to crop up long after their phonetic role had disappeared.

The changes in the futhark also mark an increased stress on the staves as a system of conventional writing as opposed to use as ideograms or in magical formulae. This emphasis on literacy was part of the growing commercial sophistication of the North and also an attempt to secularize the runes after conversion. Both these trends tended to drive a wedge between the runes as a script and the elder tradition. As conversion took root, the elder knowledge passed away and all that remained was a system of writing.

In this book, we focus almost entirely on the Elder Futhark for a few reasons. The primary one is that it is the original expression of the runes as a complete and coherent system. As such, the Elder Futhark comes closest to its creator's intentions of serving as an authentic Germanic script while maintaining the indigenous symbols' use in divination and magic. With the advent of the Anglo-Saxon and Younger Futharks, the emphasis seems to shift away from the magical to more mundane purposes. In many cases, the reason the Elder Futhark continued to be used after the invention of the newer versions was likely for its magical and symbolic values — values which often became muddled, masked, or forgotten in the later futharks. To seek to understand the runes in the context of our ancestral heritage — as this book hopes to accomplish — we could hardly do better than study the original item.

ANCESTRAL USES

Most historical discussions about how our ancestors used the runes can be divided into two classes: those that argue the runes were a purely secular script and those that argue the runes were exclusively for magic or ritual. Jumping into either camp is a mistake for three reasons. The first is that there is overwhelming evidence that runic writing was used for everything from business letters to curses, and so the either/or position is archaeologically untenable.

The second reason to not take sides in this argument is that modern ideas about what is secular and what is religious are quite out of step with the probable worldview of our ancestors. Most modern archaeologists, for example, would label a gravestone as a secular use of the runes, but for our ancestors, the raising of such a monument was filled with religious significance. Naming a weapon and then engraving the name in runes upon the blade is another example of an act that could be filled with magical intent but would be classified as secular by modern scholars.

The last reason we should be careful about the secular/magical argument is that it focuses solely upon the staves instead of viewing the staves as part of a larger body of runelore. This body contains not only the symbolic meanings of the rune names but also the skills mentioned in several poems that are associated with runes. These include healing, protection, and weather charms that sometimes suggest staves but more often point far beyond them.

Taken as a whole, the secular/magical argument is an ineffective way to look at how our ancestors used the runes. A better perspective can be gained from taking stock of the whole body of evidence and then trying to draw some conclusions about how the runes fit into our ancestors' world.

Maker's Marks and Monuments

Runestaves were used for ownership and maker's marks, such as the Gallehus horn which bore the inscription: "I Hlewagast, Holt's son, made the horn." (Elliott, 80) Such inscriptions had, of course, the purely practical purpose of establishing ownership and origin. It should be remembered, however, that objects carry the effect of their past, their wyrd, with them as surely as people do. We need only recall the curse of Andvari's ring as an example. When ownership of an object is transferred, via gift or theft, its wyrd follows.

The idea of an object having an identity is also seen in the many spearheads that bear their names etched in runes. Names like "Tester" and "Assailant" would appear to cross the line between merely communicating a name and drawing power from the name. In other words, by naming the spear and engraving the name in runes on the blade, the owner or maker may have believed he was transferring the qualities of the name to the weapon via the runes. The naming of weapons, such as Gungnir and Tyrfingr, is known from Norse mythology and remains common to the present day, as evidenced by Davy Crockett's famed rifle Betsy.

Monument stones form a large body of inscriptions, including the fifth century CE Kylver stone which contains the oldest complete futhark. These monuments were usually raised to honor fallen kinsmen, such as the Gripsholm stone that reads: "Tolla had this stone raised after her son, Haraldr, Ingvar's brother. They travelled valiantly far for gold, and in the east gave food to the eagle. They died in the south in Sarkland (Norse word for the Middle East)." (Faulkes, 231) This is the type of stone referred to in the *Havamal* as being "by kith raised over kinsmen." (st. 72) Monuments had the secular purpose of helping to ease the grief, and possibly raise the prestige, of the relative who raised the stone. Such monuments could also serve as a constant reminder of common identity and heritage for those who lived near them.

The attitude of our ancestors toward their dead kinsmen should be considered when examining these stones. The living felt a continuing relationship with the dead and left offerings near grave mounds and memorial stones. These offerings were intended to encourage a positive feeling among the dead, and some stones seem to have had a similar purpose. An example is the ninth century Gorlev stone from Zealand which reads: "Thjodvi raised this stone for Odinkar. FutharkhniastblmR. Enjoy your memorial well. Thistill mistill kistill. I set the runes rightly." (Elliott, 84) The runes in this case would seem to both bear a message and aid in its conveyance through the use of magical formulae.

Runakefli and Bracteates

Another large body of surviving runic inscriptions occurs on sticks or pieces of bark preserved in bogs or other oxygen-free environments. This type of artifact, collectively called runakefli, has been found across Northern Europe, but most of them are from sites in Bergen, Norway, and Novgorod, Russia. Runakefli are spoken of in several of the family sagas, Saxo's *Danish History*, the late Icelandic magical manuscript *Galdrabok*, and the sixth century correspondence of Venantius Fortunatus, Bishop of Poitiers.

Surviving inscriptions convey a dizzying variety of messages from business letters ("Thorkel Moneyer sends you pepper" (Faulkes, 234)) to commands from impatient wives ("Gyda says you are to go home" (Elliott, 92)) to pleas for love ("My darling kiss me" (ibid.)) to well wishes ("Be you hale and in good spirits. Thorr receive you. Odin own you." (Faulkes, 236)). The evidence of these runakefli points to the conclusion that runes were used for every imaginable purpose during the Viking Age, and it would be no great leap to assume similar uses by the continental Germans prior to or soon after their conversion.

Many runakefli have inscriptions of single staves or nonsensical formulae, and these inscriptions are mirrored by similar inscriptions on bracteates and elsewhere. The Lindholm amulet displays a runic inscription of, in order, eight Ansuz, three Algiz, three Nauthiz, one Berkano, one Mannaz, one Uruz, three Tiwaz, and then the ubiquitous "magic word" Ansuz-Laguz-Uruz. While it could be argued that such an inscription is decorative or indicative of some meaning we cannot discern, it seems far more likely that the Lindholm inscription was intended to carry the power of the runes in the manner recited in the magical formulae of *Sigrdrifumal*.

To inscriptions like the Lindholm amulet can be added the numerous complete futharks engraved on objects as varied as runakefli, swords, amulets, and stones. Even more explicit is a bracteate from Zealand that reads: "I am called Hariuha, one who knows about dangerous things. I bring luck." (Elliott, 83). The evidence points toward a belief in the talismanic power of such inscriptions, and this assumption is strengthened by the repeated occurrence of such words as "ALU," meaning luck or well-being.

Evidence of runes being used to help is matched by evidence of a belief in their power to hurt. *Egil's Saga* gives a detailed account of how Egil carved runes on a "scorn pole" (*nidstang*) that cursed King Eirik Bloodaxe, and *Grettir's Saga* recounts the curse of a witch carved onto a tree trunk. The *Havamal* mentions spells carved on a "gnarled root" (st. 151), and the late *Galdrabok* is full of runic mischief intended to cause misfortune, sickness, and even flatulence. It is almost certainly spells such as these that are meant in *Voluspa* when the seeress claims that Heidr "practiced ganda" (st. 22). Ganda is a type of conjuring associated with gandr sticks, which are apparently a type of runakefli.

It is difficult for us to look back and understand exactly what our ancestors thought about such practices. We do know that the belief in the efficacy of "rune magic" persisted after conversion. The existence of the *Galdrabok* confirms it, as does a passage in Bede where a man is asked if he possesses "loosening runes" (*alysendlecan runa*) on his person after his manacles fell off. This was written nearly a century after conversion.

The question of how our ancestors thought such things work still remains. We can perhaps get a glimpse of their mind-set if we remember that reference to runes does not always mean runestaves. When Odin recounts his skills in *Havamal*, he makes only passing reference to staves. *Grogaldr* lists a similar set of magical feats but does not mention staves at all. Odin often relates his skills to songs or verses, and we might have a glimpse of such songs in the Merseburg charms. This type of magic seems to be independent of, or only peripherally related to, runestaves, and so it would appear to rely on the idea or concept of the rune for its power.

The type of magic described above can be contrasted with the list of magical skills in *Sigrdrifumal*. The valkyrie relates nearly every feat of magic to carved staves. These staves seem to be part of larger magical formulae that she only hints at, but there can be no doubt the staves play a clear role. This can be compared to the episode in *Egil's Saga* where Egil foils an attempt to poison him by cutting runes and singing a verse. It would appear that the runestave points toward something or acts as a focal point for something beyond the stave itself. It can perhaps be concluded that this "something" is the larger idea of the rune itself and is the same source of power the magic in the previous paragraph seeks to access.

Rune Divination

No discussion of our ancestors' use of the runes is complete without mention of divination and the fascinating passage in *Germania* where Tacitus describes the ancient process:

To divination and lots they pay attention beyond any other people. Their method of casting lots is a simple one: they cut a bough from a fruit-bearing tree and divide it into small pieces; these they mark with certain distinguishing signs and scatter at random and without order over a white cloth. Then, after invoking the gods and with eyes lifted up to heaven, the priest of the community, if the lots are consulted publicly, or, if privately, the father of the family, takes up three pieces one at a time and interprets them according to the signs previously marked on them. (Germania, 31)

The fancy word for this type of divination process is "sortilege," and the description above provides explicit detail about divination rituals only hinted at elsewhere. These hints are numerous. Beowulf and his companions observe the omens (*hael sceawedon*) before sailing to Denmark. Bede mentions the casting of lots, as do other Old English poets. *Voluspa* tells us of the wyrd "scored on wood" by the Norns, (st. 20) and that Hoenir will handle the "blood wood" (hlut vid) again after Ragnarok. (st. 62) In

Hymiskvitha stanza 1, the gods "shook twigs" (*hristu teina*) to determine their next course of action. This poetic evidence lends credence to the consultation of the "stave oracle" in *Heimskringla* 42 and the drawing of lots that costs King Vikar his life in *Gautrek's Saga*. Besides Tacitus, both Caesar and Plutarch mention the Germanic practice of sortilege.

The list of literary references above gives credence to Tacitus' statement that the Germans paid great attention to divination. It should also be remembered that the Romans were nearly obsessed with omens and auguries, and so Tacitus' stress on how important this practice was to our ancestors probably means that divination played a huge role in the decision-making processes of the Germanic tribes.

It has been correctly noted by many commentators that Tacitus does not use the word "rune" in his description, and we therefore are not certain that this process involved the Elder Futhark or any other known group of runestaves. Two points, however, argue in favor of the runes being the signs Tacitus described. The first point is that Tacitus wrote in Latin. The word "rune" would have been unknown to him, and its absence should therefore be no surprise. The phrase translated as "certain distinguishing signs" is "*notis quibusdam discretos.*" (Elliott, 85) Though it only contains three words, the phrase defies direct English translation. It implies both particular signs as opposed to random ones and the idea that these signs had meaning, perhaps even a predetermined one.

Tacitus' wording seems to point to a symbolic system, and the fact that the runes are the only system of this type known to exist among our ancestors is the second argument in their favor. In short, we should ask ourselves which is more likely: that our ancestors used runes for divination or that they used a second, unknown system of which no literary mention is made and no archaeological evidence remains? The obvious answer is that they used runes.

Assuming that runes were used for divination, what can we learn about both the runes and our ancestors from the process Tacitus describes? The first thing we can learn about the runes is that the deeper, symbolic meaning of the rune-name was important because it is this meaning that would have been central to the interpretation process. Casting runes was not like flipping a coin for yes/no answers. Instead, the relevance and meaning of the stave that was drawn had to be puzzled out, and the knowledge to solve this puzzle can only have come from an understanding of the symbolic meaning attached to each stave.

The process also gives us clues about how our ancestors viewed the concepts of time and fate. The drawing of three runes described by Tacitus has led many to conclude that our ancestors looked to the Norns when consulting the runes. This idea is borne out by Caesar's statement that when casting lots the Germans looked to the "*matres familiae*" ("mothers of the family"), a triad of female deities that can perhaps be equated with the Norns. (Elliott, 85) The involvement of the Norns implies that the concept of wyrd was central to the divination process. This could mean that our ancestors looked at the course of events as a progression that could be affected as opposed to being arbitrarily predetermined. Fate was both knowable and changeable to those who could unravel its mysteries, and the runes provided the ideal tool for doing so.

Comparing this divination process with other known rituals can also offer insight. Our ancestors were known to observe the outcomes of single combat, the paths of running animals, the screams of tortured prisoners, or the behavior of special horses to gain insight into the "counsel of the gods." (*Germania*, 110) Reading the runes, however, is different. Rather than attempting to access or interpret the will or opinion of a deity, rune divination seeks to understand the flow of cause and effect as it is manifested in wyrd and made discernible through the runes. This is the process the gods themselves are said to use, and it speaks of a people determined to understand their world and master their destiny. Instead of seeking knowledge of a fate they would be forced to accept, readers of the runes sought insight into how they could best shape their future.

Conclusions

With all of the above information in mind, we can return to the question of how our ancestors used the runes. The magical or mundane question can be dismissed, as evidence from business letters to runic curses shows. Our ancestors used runes for such a wide array of reasons that no simple system can be constructed to describe these purposes.

What we can be sure about is that the runes played a huge role in our ancestors' world. They were used to correspond with friends, curse enemies, charm loved ones, continue relationships with dead kinsmen, and channel power into weapons. They were used by gods and men to delve the wyrd of the world, and a knowledge of their mysteries was believed to give men a heightened ability to affect the world.

Think of the space in our own world filled by literacy, prayer, philosophy, and science. This is the space that was filled by the runes in the minds of our ancestors. This space was certainly different in scope and shape in their society, but it was still undoubtedly vast.

MODERN USES

Conversion did not immediately erase the runes from the culture of the northlands. In fact, many of the stone monuments in Scandinavia and Britain were raised after conversion, and the vast majority of runakefli are also from this period. Even as the runes slowly gave ground to the Roman alphabet, knowledge of the staves and their meanings never completely disappeared. This is fortunate for modern Heathens, because it offers us a unique window into the culture and ideology of our ancestors, and more importantly, it allows us to use ancestral tools to help us understand the ways of our people.

Modern Heathen usage of the runes is different in many ways from the practices of our ancestors. These modern uses vary widely among Heathens, and this variation is perfectly legitimate. Despite the differences, each modern use should be predicated on a solid understanding of the runes and their place in our culture. Using runes in place of the Tarot or I Ching might be chic in some circles, and assigning meaning to the runes from the principles of Kabbala probably seems much easier than figuring it out for yourself, but these things do not belong to our folk. Whatever uses we put the runes to today, they must be rooted in the wisdom of our ancestors to be Heathen.

Identity and Confidence

Perhaps the simplest and most eloquent modern use of the runes is as a mark of identity. Such uses can be as simple as writing our names or other English words on a T-shirt in runes or as complex and meaningful as inscribing the entire futhark on a bowl used in blot. Runic tattoos and the rune banners used by some Heathen groups also fall into this category.

Using the runes to write in English is very straightforward. Most people start out with simple transliteration, that is, substituting runes one-for-one with Roman letters. As comfort grows, dropping double letters and silent letters brings us closer to the way our ancestors wrote with runes. Another important tool is to use the staves that represent sounds that use multiple letters, like Thursaz for "th" and Inguz for "ing."

Remember that our ancestors wrote phonetically; in other words, it is the sound value that matters, not the Roman letters used to write the word in English. For example, the word "who" could be written ᚹᚺᛟ but if we drop the silent "w" and realize the vowel sounds more like a "u" than an "o," we get ᚺᚢ.

Vowel sounds are tough because English has more vowels than the futhark, which is one reason why the Old English rune-row expanded, but remember that there are no standard spellings for runic writing. A single word would often be spelled two or three different ways in the same inscription. Be creative and personalize your technique; our ancestors certainly did.

Writing with runes requires only a basic understanding of runic phonetic values, but it speaks to something deeper. The runes belong to us. They are a legacy of our ancestry, and when we use them in almost any way, we are not only proudly proclaiming our identity to the world, we are also consciously reaching back toward the culture and wisdom of our ancestors.

This concept points directly to the similar idea of using the runes for confidence or good luck. Runakefli that wish good luck on the owner and amulets inscribed with runes can meet many of the same needs for modern Heathens as they did for our ancestors. Any dismissal of such charms as mere superstition overlooks the effect that confidence and positive attitude can have in our lives.

If, for example, a Heathen faces a difficult journey or task that he must confront alone, carrying a runakefli that his Heathen kinsmen made him for good luck will remind him that he is not truly alone. Remembering his people and his ancestors will build his confidence and help him face his task with courage. The good luck that is likely to follow does not rely on magic; it draws on the power of our way and our people.

Blot

Blot is the central ritual in Heathenry. It is usually offered to mark the progression of the seasons, but it can also be done to commemorate special occasions. For our ancestors, blot involved the sacrifice of animals and ritual feasting, often over a series of days.

In modern Heathenry, blot is usually offered with ritual toasts and rarely lasts more than an hour, even in larger groups. Though different Heathen groups use different methods for blot, most follow a similar series of steps, and runes often play a role in several of these steps.

The first place where runes are often used in blot is in the process of creating a sacred space. Our ancestors usually had traditional places to hold blot, such as a hof or grove. Custom and long usage created a sense of purpose when our ancestors gathered in these sacred places. Modern Heathens rarely have comparable holy places, and so we must create the space each time we blot.

There are several methods for creating sacred space, and they are often used together (see *Heathen Handbook*, Sec. VIII). One common method that uses runes is the chanting of the futhark as the participants walk in a circle around the ground where the blot is to be held. Usually, one person says the names of the runes and the group repeats after him.

A similar method that uses runes to help create sacred space is the chanting of three rune names three times. These runes are usually related to the specific blot. Both these methods are intended to focus the group on the ritual and create a sense of unity and common purpose.

Runes can also be used later in the blot to help the group concentrate on the meaning of the blot. This can take the form of group meditation on a rune related to the purpose of the blot. For example, the feminine fertility aspect of an Ostara blot can be paired with meditation on Berkano, or the heritage theme of a Winter Nights blot can be brought into focus with meditation on Othala. An alternative to meditation could be each person briefly stating how the rune helps them relate to the blot. Either of these processes should help the group concentrate on the ritual.

The use of runes to help focus during blot can greatly enhance the ritual experience. Heathens should not be afraid to experiment with different practices that help them both better understand the runes and offer more meaningful blot.

Meditation

Runic meditation is an idea that has not received adequate attention in the context of Heathenry. Unfortunately, it has been the object of attempts to slap a runic gloss on top of Buddhist or other foreign meditation techniques. Books and articles on everything from rune mantras to rune yoga are all too easy to find, but we have to ask ourselves if we can graft techniques and ideas from alien creeds into our way and still call it Heathenry.

In terms of meditation, the conflict stems from differences in worldview. Heathenry focuses on the improvement of the individual within the context of his folk. Ours is a very action-oriented and reality-centered way of life. We do not reject the physical world or our role in it. Instead, we embrace our lives as a great challenge to be worthy of the bloodgift of our ancestors. Any techniques or ideology that requires us to withdraw from the world, reject our identity, or dismiss our will and deeds as futile is not compatible with Heathenry.

Most of the meditation techniques imported from the East are premised on the ideas that the world is an illusion that must be rejected to reach enlightenment and that our identity as a person is the key obstacle that must be overcome on the path toward this transcendent experience. The goal of the extinction of the ego is, in terms of meditation, worked toward through a variety of techniques that center on the "emptying of the mind," and in this perfect stillness and nothingness, enlightenment is sought.

The ideas in the above paragraph run so counter to the basic tenets of Heathenry that it should be obvious they have no place in our way. We must look to our own traditions to find the keys to understanding a Heathen method for focusing our mind on an idea or purpose.

Examples from the lore are not hard to find. The story of the Icelandic lawspeaker who went "under his cloak" when contemplating conversion to Christianity can be compared to tales of men and women sitting all night on the graves of ancestors seeking inspiration. These examples share the attributes of solitude, quiet, and concentration in pursuit of wisdom or understanding that is applicable to our lives. In fact, Heathen meditation would be more accurately referred to as "concentration," as it is not an emptying of the mind but an intense focus on the goal at hand.

Modern runic concentration should follow the same path. The elements of solitude, quiet, and comfort are essential. Mental focus cannot be easily achieved amid distraction, so meditation requires that you find a place that you can practice in peace.

Our ancestors usually went outdoors, but this was probably more due to small and cramped living spaces than a desire to be closer to nature. If peace and quiet is more accessible indoors, then stay inside. Find a place where temperature and noise are not a problem. Take care of hunger, thirst, and other bodily functions that can distract, then get into a comfortable position and prepare to think.

It should also be remembered that our ancestors' practice was not centered around "not thinking of anything." Emptying the mind or the paradoxical have no place in our way. For us, the purpose can be as specific as an immediate decision regarding family or career, or it can be as general as seeking to bring yourself toward the ways of our ancestors. The goal is to focus.

For runic concentration, choose a rune that relates to your purpose. This rune can be selected randomly or intentionally. Some Heathens move methodically through the futhark; others use the divination process that will be discussed later. Concentration can begin by focusing on the image of the stave to clear and settle the mind for the work at hand. When this is done, think about the meaning of the rune and how it relates to your purpose. Guide your thinking through the connections that bind the rune to both your ancestors and your own life.

The key is to balance mental focus with letting new ideas and perspectives bubble to the surface. It takes practice to stay on topic while not being too rigid. If done regularly, both skill and comfort in the process will grow. Do not expect immediate revelation. Returning to the same questions is not a sign of failure; it is an indication of perseverance and dedication.

Remember that the goal is understanding, and this takes both contemplation and the integration of our thoughts into the reality of our world. Ideas that occur during concentration are meaningful only if they impact how we live our lives. We are not seeking the secrets of the cosmos or some sublime transcendence. Heathen "meditation" should help us be wiser and live closer to the ways of our ancestors.

A Method of Study

The method used to develop the meanings of the runes in this book was simple. A week was dedicated to each rune. The etymology of the rune-name was used as a starting point as well as what the rune-poems had to say about the stave. Other historical sources were incorporated where relevant. The idea was to determine what the rune meant to our ancestors, then use that understanding as a base on which to build. The essence of Heathenry is found in our history and identity; our past provides the foundation from which we reach into the future.

Next, an investigation into the lore (Eddas, sagas, etc.) was made pertaining to the rune in question. On a few occasions, references to specific staves are made in the *Poetic Edda* (namely Thurisaz, Nauthiz, and Tiwaz), but in every case the concept embodied by each stave can easily be found in the lore. This proved useful in trying to comprehend traditional applications of the runes. If we can grasp the reason why our ancestors employed a certain stave, that should serve as a guide for putting modern runic "apps" to work.

Third, associations between the runes themselves were looked into. Often the futhark is deliberately ordered so that each stave has obvious ties to the runes immediately before and after it. Other connections are more subtle and require abstract thinking to illuminate. Seeing how pairs or groups of runes work together provides valuable insight that one would otherwise lack when considering them only as individual staves.

Finally, the collected information was projected forward to determine what the runes mean to the folk today. For this endeavor, the practice of concentration described above proved especially useful, and it is recommended that our readers also make use of this method. For the futhark to remain a vital, living system, the runes must serve a purpose in the lives of modern Heathens, just as they did for our ancestors. Only by following Odin's example and claiming them for ourselves can we hope to carry on the runic tradition and pass this part of our heritage on to the next generation.

Fehu

Fehu (fay-hoo) cattle, wealth. Fehu can be traced to OHG *fihu* and ultimately to PIE *peku*, both meaning "cattle." It later came to mean wealth in general but specifically chattel — moveable possessions.

Fehu also means wealth or money in the rune-poems, all of which warn against greed. In our ancestors' world there was no better measure of personal wealth than the number of cattle or other livestock an individual owned. Wealth to them was not a measure of status symbols or material goods but of the basic necessities of life — food, clothing, and shelter. Cattle provided all of these things and were thus the ultimate renewable resource.

Tacitus says of the Germanic tribes that "cattle are their sole, greatly prized wealth," but the same could be said of his home state of Rome. Just as the English word "fee" comes from the same root as Fehu, the Roman word for money, *pecunia*, derives from the Latin *pecus*, "cattle." Some scholars believe the concept of charging interest on money actually arose from observing the natural increase in livestock. In other words, a cow borrowed one year would equal a repayment of a cow and a calf the next.

In our lore, Fehu can be connected to Audhumbla, the primal cow that nourishes the first giant, Ymir, and frees the first god from the ice. Fehu matches Audhumbla well as it not only means "cattle" but is also the "primal" or first rune of the futhark. This rune also has ties to the god Frey. Aside from having the first aett (family or clan) of eight runes named in his honor, Frey has close connections to cattle.

In his role as "Lord of the Meadow" (see Inguz), Frey acts as patron deity of livestock and is thus associated with prosperity, fertility, and wealth. Tacitus mentions that cattle pulled the wagon of the ancient earth goddess Nerthus, who is believed to be the wife of Njord and the mother of Frey and Freyja. This points to a relationship between Fehu and the Vanic deities in general.

Fehu can also be found in Celtic lore, as several of the Irish myths concern cattle raids. On May 1st, the start of summer for Celtic peoples, all the cattle were driven between two fires so the smoke could purify them for a productive year. On November 1st, the beginning of winter, the livestock were culled except for those animals set aside to repopulate the herds the next year. The blood shed from slaughtering the livestock attracted the spirits of the dead, so this rune may have been useful for necromancy and divination.

Fehu has connections to several other runes. The first is to Uruz, the aurochs. As the wild ox, Uruz represents the unfettered beast in its natural state. Regarding mankind , the German philosopher Friedrich Nietzsche would relate this to what he calls the Dionysian — the impulse to embrace our inner animal and return to nature. Fehu, on the other hand, equates with Nietzsche's Apollonian — the desire to create order, law, and stability.

This drive arises from Ansuz, the bloodgift of Odin and his brothers that differentiates the ancestors from other hominids. Put simply, Fehu is our ability to self-control, to rein in our emotions and instincts in order to make a rational choice.

Fehu is also closely tied to Othala, one's inherited property. For our ancestors, this referred to the house and lands that belonged to the family and could not be traded or sold. By contrast, Fehu symbolizes "movable" property that has individual ownership and can be used however that person sees fit.

The emergence of personal property rights can be traced at least back to the Chalcolithic (c. 3200-2200 BCE) in Europe, as individual burial began to replace communal burial. The appearance of grave goods also reflected the emerging status of the individual and represented a paradigm shift in culture at that time. It should be kept in mind, however, that while people were buried separately, their remains were still laid to rest at a family site on the ancestral (odal) lands.

For Heathens, we are born into a blood line, we die into the blood line, and in our lives we represent our family with honor and pride.

The idea of Fehu is every bit as important to us today as it was to our ancestors. Although few of us equate cattle with wealth, those who raise livestock or trade commodities still make that connection. But for those who have never been on a ranch or to a feed yard, Fehu can be thought of as disposable or "liquid" wealth — any assets not tied up in houses or real estate that can be spent or exchanged easily.

Fehu money can be thought of as magic. As any economist will tell you, a $100 bill in itself is worthless. It is only the belief we place in an abstract idea (money) that gives it value. As we move ever closer to a cashless society our belief in Fehu has grown to the point that even physical representations (paper money) are being replaced by intangible ones such as credit cards, PayPal accounts, and Bitcoin.

These innovations are necessary to operate in the modern world, but have come with a price. To Prime a new flatscreen to your Visa is easier and more convenient than bringing a cow to the store to exchange for the TV, even though it amounts to roughly the same thing. The convenience of money allows economies to grow and operate smoothly; however, it is also easier to be irresponsible with a credit card than it is to trade off a living being that has been part of your family. As one can imagine, "impulse buying" did not present much of a problem to our ancestors, nor did they seek to find meaning in their lives through empty materialism.

For modern Heathens, the positive aspects of Fehu thus represent making rational decisions as opposed to rash ones, taking the long road of delayed gratification versus the convenience of instant gratification, and being a responsible overseer of resources instead of wasting them.

Uruz

Uruz (oor-ooz) aurochs. Uruz has remained almost unchanged dating back to Proto-Indo-European. It means "aurochs," a giant wild ox that went extinct throughout most of Europe a thousand years ago. Hunting this creature was an ordeal for our ancient ancestors and Neanderthals alike. Many Neanderthal remains bear evidence that they died from injuries that were likely inflicted while hunting, leading many anthropologists to believe they had close contact with aurochs.

Among the Germanic tribes the hunting of the aurochs was a rite of passage for boys entering adulthood. A boy could not assume the role of a man, a provider, until he had taken part in the slaying of this beast and brought back one of its horns. Several Roman historians, from Caesar to Pliny to Tacitus, have commented on the speed and strength of these animals and consequently the symbolic value to our ancestors of killing one.

Some scholars have suggested that Uruz represents "manly strength," a meaning that carried on even after the aurochs was gone. As Ralph Elliott points out, we understand the terrible power that a dragon represents and the courage needed to face one even though we have never seen such a creature; the aurochs filled this same role in our ancestors' minds for generations after its demise. For this reason the OE rune-poem kept "aurochs" for Uruz, but the later ON and OI poems replaced it with similar sounding words that meant "slag" (the refuse from smelting iron) and "drizzle."

Uruz does not have an obvious association with any figure in our lore. The nearest parallel would be to the Fenris wolf, the monstrous beast that Tyr sacrificed his hand to bind. The wolf had grown so huge that it posed a danger to the gods, so the Aesir had a magical fetter made that could restrain him. Smelling a trap, Fenris agreed to let himself be tied up only if one of the gods would place their hand in his jaws as a pledge. Tyr volunteered to do so knowing that his sword hand would be eaten, but it was the only way the threat could be averted.

Fenris symbolizes the selfish desires that threaten the future existence of our folk. As a god of war, Tyr sets the example for other warriors to follow — he sacrifices his fighting hand in service to the folk. Rather than lord over his kin and clan to satisfy personal wants, he chooses to do what is best for all. Tyr is the wolf, but he binds that part of his nature — the wild, self-centered, childish id — for the greater good of his people.

The rite of passage of slaying the aurochs represents the same idea — the boy kills his childish desires by putting his life on the line to protect and provide for his people. In sacrificing that part of himself for the folk he partakes in the very nature of Tyr, and thus takes on the role of the true warrior.

Uruz can also be seen in its relation to the berserker fury. Meaning "bear shirt," a berserker was a warrior who would either fight naked or wear an animal skin into battle to transform himself into a wild beast. Many of the sagas speak of such men, and they are commonly associated with the cult of Odin. Our lore leaves the impression that berserkers were fearsome weapons when turned against an enemy, but their fury quickly became a liability amongst kith and kin. In other words, Fenris makes a great attack dog, but you would not let a wolf loose in your house or near your children.

The Uruz fury can thus be useful when directed outside the garth, but inside the beast must be bound so that we face friends and family as civilized animals.

Another way to consider Uruz is through its relationship to Fehu. As "cattle," Fehu is the tamed beast, the animal trained to the will of man. Uruz, our unfettered animal nature, stands in stark contrast to the discipline of Fehu, the self-control that makes civilization possible. But whereas man is the master of his livestock and the decider of their fate, the unbreakable spirit of Uruz defies any attempt to control it. As Caesar comments, the aurochs, "even if caught very young, cannot be tamed or accustomed to human beings." The only way man can determine its fate is to hunt it and kill it, and in so doing, he risks his own life.

The hunting of the aurochs is a test of wills in which there can only be one victor. Any close encounter with the beast is a near-death experience from which a man cannot emerge unchanged. The trial of Uruz can thus be seen as a metaphor for life itself — the process of "growing up" is nothing more than learning to bind our destructive nature

51

so that we may live and prosper in community with other human beings.

Uruz can also be compared to Ehwaz, the horse. While Fehu serves as an adequate analogy to the willfully bound man in society, the horse represents a more independent beast that still harbors the urge to break free. Ehwaz thus walks a finer line between wild and tame.

For our ancient ancestors, Uruz brings to mind the role of the shaman, the individual who dwelt at the edge of society and occupied the liminal area between civilization and the natural world. His ecstatic trances were a temporary unbinding of conscious control that unleashed the subconscious Uruz forces. In this sense, the shaman's ecstasy and the berserker's fury are merely different channels of the same energy, and it should come as no surprise that the shaman also belongs to Odin.

Through the wonders of DNA technology, efforts are being made to resurrect the aurochs from extinction. And while the possibility of this species being the first to ever return to the earth looks promising, the likelihood that we will ever hunt it as our ancestors did is remote. Fortunately, it is not necessary for us to literally kill an aurochs in order to become well-adjusted adults; there are other ways for us to bind our inner Fenris. Unfortunately, our modern consumer culture offers no clear path or distinction from the selfish child to the folkish man. The burden is on us as Heathens to make the psychological jump from eternal children in the global toy store to responsible adults in our local communities and tribes. Uruz today thus represents crossing that abyss — the challenge of evolving into the men and women that we can and should be.

Thurisaz

Thurisaz (thoor-i-saz) giant. Thurisaz means "thurs" (giant).

In our lore, giants symbolize the raw, chaotic forces of nature. For example, many giants have names such as "glacier" or "bitter cold." The nine giant maidens who gave birth to Heimdall are ocean waves, and the sea itself is the domain of the giant Aegir and his wife Ran. Old Norse has two words for "giant:" jotun — a neutral term for those who are sometimes the allies of gods and men (such as Mimir); and thurs — a negative term that refers to the sworn enemies of the Aesir. Thurs is often translated as "ogre" and preceded by hrim (ice) or berg (mountain) and often described as having three or more heads. Grimm finds cognates for jotun and thurs in Gothic that are associated with eating and drinking, thus pointing to giants as creatures with endless appetites. This fits with what we know about their nature, as they are often depicted as "eating up" the resources of gods and men. In *Gylfaginning* ch. 46, giants out-eat and out-drink Loki and Thor despite the best efforts of the Aesir.

To say that giants play a large role in our lore is both an understatement and a bad pun. *Voluspa* tells how the first living creature in the universe was the thurs Ymir, and it is from him that all other giants are descended. Saxo backs up the claim that giants are the oldest beings: "The first (race) were creatures of monstrous size far surpassing humans in bodily stature." One only needs to stand at the edge of the ocean, survive a blizzard, or scale a mountain to feel the sense of awe that these ancient giants inspire.

Thurisaz is one of the few staves specifically mentioned in the Eddas. In *Skirnismal* st. 36, Frey's friend Skirnir coerces the giantess Gerd into accepting Frey's marriage proposal by threatening to carve Thurisaz on her in addition to casting three spells: "madness, weeping, and anxiety." What he intends with this triple curse is to break any Fehu bonds of restraint that Gerd may possess, thus enslaving her forever to her giant nature and rendering her unfit to live in civilized society. Gerd, a tolerable jotun, would be condemned to life as a hated thurs. As Skirnir puts it, "to the frost-thurs' hall shall you each day creep without choice… you shall weep because men have such loathing against you."

In our ancestors' world, no punishment was more severe than being shunned from one's community, so Gerd agrees to marry Frey rather than face such a terrible consequence.

In the OE rune-poem the name Thurisaz was replaced by "Thorn." This was probably chosen because of the shape of the runestave, but the reason for changing it was likely to remove Heathen influence from the OE futhorc. Whereas the ON and OI rune-poems refer to giants as "torturers of women," the OE version reads: "Thorn is painfully sharp to any warrior/ seizing it is bad, excessively severe/ for any person who lies among them." While this retains the idea of an element of nature harmful to man, it also demythologizes our world by replacing a living force with a lifeless "thing." The giants, while often hostile, are a vital part of the environment that we must struggle to maintain balance with.

Our view of the earth as a living system stands in sharp contrast to the mundane, dead land that the desert god gives Adam "dominion" over. The Church's battle to sever our ancestors' connection with the living earth carried on for centuries, yet we have never completely surrendered the idea that our soil is sacred.

As late as the end of the 14th century a three-headed thurs appears in *The Canterbury Tales*, although by that time Chaucer admits that Christian friars "thick as dust in a sunbeam" have run the elves, fairies, and other wights off the land. Today it is our sacred duty to bring them back.

Unlike most staves, the "thorn" rune continued to be used in England even after the switch was made to the Roman alphabet. Because Latin has no "th" sound, it lacks a symbol to represent it, so people kept using Thorn for this purpose. Since letters were more often written than carved by then, the sharp point of Thorn was gradually rounded so that it came to resemble a lower-case "p" only with a taller stem. Through the Middle Ages its shape further evolved to look more and more like a "y" until the two symbols were identical. Thus we find "ye" in Middle English (as in "ye" old pub) instead of our modern "the."

Another way to look at Thurisaz is in relation to the rune that precedes it. Just as Uruz is the untamed beast, Thurisaz is the uncontrollable power of nature. But as we are ourselves animals, we hold the force of Uruz within us. It symbolizes the struggle to fetter our inner Fenris so that our god-like nature can shine through (see Ansuz). Thurisaz, however, represents the external struggle with the forces of the world that work against us. Both these runes remind us of the battles we must fight daily, some within our own minds and others in the world outside.

Today, Thurisaz is often associated with Thor. This is due largely to modern authors who attempt to connect a deity to each and every rune as well as the obvious similarity between "Thor" and "thurs." As the slayer of giants, Thor does have clear ties to Thurisaz, but in this case the god represents the "negative" polarity of the rune. Thurisaz is the chaotic, destructive forces at work in our world; Thor is the reverse of that, the power we have to bring order to our lives so that people can prosper.

For our ancestors, Thurisaz meant natural hazards like nasty weather or the perils of crossing the open sea (thus the invocations to Thor to calm the wind and waves that occur in the sagas). Modern science has given us the advantages of early alert systems and safer means of travel to lessen the impact that such giants would have on us. Natural disasters still strike with deadly force, but in most cases the giants of old are mere inconveniences in this day and age.

Does this mean that we have conquered Thurisaz? Hardly. Giants still threaten our existence, but now they operate in more subtle and symbolic ways. TV, the internet, even video games can occasionally be used for our benefit (jotuns), but far more often these tools are abused, feeding destructive desires for escapism and further distancing us from our goals (thurses). Thurisaz thus represents those things that are a "thorn" in our side, anything that holds us back as individuals or as a community: addictions, distractions, egoism, materialism, ignorance, negative self-images, etc.

Ansuz

Ansuz (an-sooz) god. Ansuz can be traced back to PIE *ansu* — "god, spirit, or demon." It is related to the Hittite word *hassus* which meant "king" or "sovereign god." In the OI rune poem, it is specifically tied to Odin as "Lord of Valhalla" and "the ancient creator."

In the OE poem Ansuz was replaced by *oss*, "mouth of a river." Some scholars have argued that this change can still be seen as a reference to Odin/Woden as "the source of speech and wisdom," which may be true; however, as we saw with Thurisaz, this was another move intended to divorce the runes from their Heathen essence. The runes are a crucial part of our heritage, a legacy entrusted to us by our ancestors. We prove ourselves worthy of this gift by scraping away the alien influence of the Church and seeking the meaning of the runes as closely to the original source as possible.

Ansuz in our lore is closely connected to Odin. As leader of the Aesir and the patron deity of kings and warriors, Odin wields incredible power over people and events. This power does not arise from brute strength but from the vast knowledge he sacrifices himself on the World Tree to gain.

Today we think of "sacrifice" as giving something up or destroying it, but our ancestors understood this term in its original sense — to make something holy. Odin does not give up his life on the Tree in pursuit of a selfish goal to be a rune-master, ruler of the gods, or decider of fates; rather, he becomes all these things because he has dedicated his life to a higher purpose — the preservation of his people through the difficult times that lie ahead. Every move Odin makes in Midgard, every warrior he takes to Valhalla, everything he risks and suffers is designed to help the sacred cause of staving off Ragnarok. This ability to look into the future, see the forces that oppose you, and make the necessary sacrifices to overcome them is the power of Ansuz.

The association of Ansuz with Odin's abilities also ties this stave to magic. At the end of *Havamal*, Odin lists his eighteen runes — "nine mighty spells" he learns from Mimir after sacrificing himself on Yggdrasil and nine more we assume he gains by pledging his eye to the Well for another drink of Odroerir. All of these involve the Ansuz power of altering one's environment in accordance with the rune-master's will.

The uses of these magical charms run the gamut from healing and protection to necromancy and love spells, but each requires an element of conscious control over nature, other people, or one's self. Archaeological evidence also points to the importance of Ansuz in magical formulas. The Lindholm (Sweden) amulet displays an inscription of twenty-four runes, which is likely symbolic of the power of the entire futhark. Rather than containing each rune in sequence (as is common on many inscriptions), this amulet begins with eight Ansuz staves in a row and ends with the magic word ALU (Ansuz-Laguz-Uruz).

Using Ansuz a total of nine times is not likely to be a coincidence as this number is itself associated with Odin and magic. Odin spends nine nights hanging from Yggdrasil and is again suspended between fires for nine nights in *Grimnismal*. Rune spells almost always occur in groups of nine, as can be seen in *Havamal*, *Sigrdrifumal*, *Rigsthula*, and *Grogaldr*. This number means more in our lore than a literal count though — it symbolizes both a multitude and a completion.

For example, we are told there are "nine worlds" of Yggdrasil, but the names of several more can be found in the Eddas. By "nine," then, we understand there are many worlds in the Tree (a multitude) and that the Tree contains all possible worlds (a completion).

Although the name of the Ansuz stave was Christianized to Os in the OE rune-poem, its connection to Odin, magic, and the number nine lived on in the "Nine Herbs Charm." This protective spell against sickness and death depicts Woden (Odin) slaying a serpent with "nine glory-twigs" so that it "flew apart into nine parts." Since Woden appears on only one other occasion in OE literature (and there in an unflattering light), people's belief in the Ansuz power of this charm must have been particularly strong for it to still be in use centuries after the conversion of Heathen England.

Ansuz can also be considered in relation to other runes. Earlier we discussed Uruz in connection to the cult of Odin as a symbol of berserker rage, the means by which these warriors unleash their inner beast. In the Eddas, this Uruz power is represented by Odin's wolves, Geri and Freki.

Odin is also pictured as having two ravens — Thought and Memory — that represent his ability to let his mind travel outside his body to the farthest reaches of Asgard. New Agers would call this "astral travel," but it is often mentioned in the sagas as a practice of northern magicians and warriors. But whereas going berserk requires pushing aside conscious control to let primal unconscious forces (Uruz) take the reins, the ability to mind-travel demands complete concentration of conscious willpower (Ansuz).

This Ansuz power can also be used in battle. In the *Saga of Hrolf Kraki*, Bodvar Bjarki fights in the form of a bear while his body remains safely inside. Thinking him asleep, another warrior breaks his concentration by shaking him, at which point the bear disappears, and the tide of battle turns against them.

The Ansuz/Uruz relationship goes further. We are complex creatures who possess both an animal nature (Uruz) and a god-like nature (Ansuz) that was given to us by Odin and his brothers. Most people use only enough of their Ansuz power to bind their inner Uruz, thus producing "individuals" who behave much like sheep or cattle: following the herd, doing what they are told, and never giving their situation a second thought. While our consumer culture thrives on people who are too complacent to develop critical thinking skills, this falls far short of our potential. The blood of the gods runs through our veins, and we belittle this divine gift by not striving to rise above the masses and emulate the example of the Aesir.

Ansuz can be thought of as the abstract reasoning abilities that differentiate man from other animals, the upward striving that drives us to achieve deeds worthy of admiration. Ansuz is consciousness itself — our ability to conceive of a new way coupled with our will to make it happen. Odin's first act of Ansuz was to slay Ymir and build a new world from his corpse. This represents not an actual murder but the overthrowing of the status quo to create a better way of life for future generations of his people.

The Odinic journey is a movement toward higher consciousness. For modern Heathens, this means bucking the trends of consumerism and complacency. We demonstrate Ansuz in our lives by becoming active in our local communities, educating ourselves, planting a garden, showing pride in our heritage, and changing our world for the better.

Raidho

Raidho (ray-doh or ray-thoh) riding, journey. Raidho
comes from the PIE root *reidh*, "to ride," and it is referred to
as "riding" in all the rune-poems. To our ancestors, this
held the obvious meaning of riding on horseback ("the toil
of the horse" in the Icelandic poem), but it held other
connotations as well. One etymology of the rune is "to
swing," and the dangling bodies of people who were
hanged were said to be "riding the gallows." This points to
Raidho being connected with the journey to Hel undertaken
by the souls of the dead and also to Odin's shamanic
death/journey on the World-Tree. It is not hard to imagine
this rune being used as a charm for the travels of both the
living and the dead.

In our lore, Raidho is closely tied to the nine-day trek to
the realm of the dead. The road to Hel is a difficult one,
thus family often buried their kin with special shoes called
Hel-shoes to protect them from dangers encountered along

the way. Even the gods are not exempt from traveling the Hel-road, as Baldr must take this trip after his death. Although the way is barred to the living, Hermod manages to make it at the behest of the gods by riding Sleipnir, the horse who serves as the ideal shamanic vehicle for moving between the worlds.

Another etymology of Raido is "wagon." Tacitus speaks of the earth goddess Nerthus, who was likely the wife of Njord and mother of Frey and Freyja, being carried around the lands of some Germanic tribes in a wagon. A similar ritual appears in the *Saga of Olaf Tryggvasson* where Frey makes an annual wagon trip around Sweden. During the procession, all weapons were put away, and feasting and frith ruled the day. The wagon seems especially connected to these Vanic gods of peace and prosperity. Their name Wanes actually means "wagon" in Anglo-Saxon.

As fertility deities, the Vanir are associated with sexual intercourse. It should come as little surprise then that Raidho also symbolizes sex. The Icelandic rune-poem calls Raidho "a sweet sitting," and the OE says it "is easy for heroes inside the hall." Our ancestors were not saddled with the sexual hang-ups so common in our culture today, and it is the pure pleasure of the act that the rune-poems emphasize. It may be that this kind of "riding" was another method of enabling one's mind to travel the worlds.

In relation to other runes, Raidho can hardly be separated from Ehwaz, the horse. "Riding" primarily refers to being on horseback, and even when used as sexual innuendo it refers to the same back-and-forth jockeying motion. In a bit of role-reversal, it was believed that a nightmare occurred when a "mare" — a malevolent spirit in the form of a horse — would ride a person in their sleep, thus causing them to suffocate, grow ill, or even die. Perhaps what our forebears had in mind was that, in the hostile world of night, the horse took its chance to be on top and enjoy the ride. This reversal would appeal to the pagan ideal of balance, especially after a journey that was "worst for the horses."

Apart from a literal horse, Ehwaz symbolizes vehicles in general, especially the shamanic vehicles encountered so often in our lore in the shapes of various animals. The forms of birds, bears, boars, wolves, whales, and others are all employed to carry the consciousness of gods and men to places they otherwise could not reach as well as to accomplish feats beyond the ability of the human body. Riding such vehicles connects Raidho to more than just Ehwaz; these two runes are part of a larger complex of ideas that includes Ansuz, the mental control of the shamanic practitioner, and Eihwaz, the World Tree that connects all possible realms in which the vehicles travel. In this sense, Raidho represents riding not outward into the physical world, but inward to explore the recesses of the mind — the ecstatic trip into altered states of consciousness.

Raidho has a close bond to at least one other rune. Above we made mention of Nerthus and her annual trek around the tribal lands. Tacitus points out that her wagon is pulled not by horses, as one might expect, but by cows. The slower movement of cattle makes them an appropriate vehicle for the earth goddess, as her journey symbolizes the long toil of growing crops and the planning involved in raising livestock. As opposed to the inner trip of Ehwaz in search of knowledge, Nerthus' external journey seeks the material blessings of fertility and prosperity. In this aspect, then, Raidho can thus be tied to Fehu as both cattle and wealth.

Even though riding horses has become more of a pastime than a means of transportation, the concept of the journey remains just as important to modern men and women. We can think of "riding" in two ways, each related to one of our ancestral pantheons. For the Vanir, the yearly journey in the wagon represented a marking of territory. More than that, it was a renewal of their relationship with the land itself, a sacred marriage without which the grass would not grow and the people could not prosper. "Riding" meant developing an intimacy with the soil that would bring forth new life. Vanic riding calls us back to our roots in the earth, a reminder that the land we live and depend on is itself alive and sacred .

While the Vanic journey defines the boundary of the garth and our special relationship to everything inside it, riding for the Aesir means leaving the safety of home to experience the larger world. In the Viking Age it was thought cowardly to be a "stay-at-home," and the rite of passage for many youths involved travel to foreign shores. It was on these journeys far from home that they connected to the cult of Odin, the god whose journeys in search of knowledge never ceased. Like Odin, travelers gain knowledge of the world, but more importantly they learn about themselves. The journey outside the garth is an initiation, a trip from which we cannot return unchanged. The Aesir's riding thus represents broadening our view of the world, challenging ourselves with new experiences, and evolving to higher physical, mental, and spiritual states.

Kenaz/Kaunaz

Kenaz/Kaunaz (kee-naz/kou-naz) torch/ulcer. The etymology of this rune can be traced to roots meaning either "torch" or "ulcer," and the rune-poems support both names. The OE poem gives its name as "torch" in the sense of illumination or a guiding light, and because this fits nicely with modern occult ideas, this is the meaning that most contemporary books offer. The ON and OI poems, however, call this rune "ulcer," which seems to be a generic term for a variety of illnesses. In Kenaz/Kaunaz, then, we have an ideal example of a rune's face-up/face-down dynamic (see APPENDIX I). In ancient inscriptions this stave is only about half the height of the others, but in later (Younger) futharks it gains full size.

Attempts have been made to relate Kenaz to Loki in our lore. Loki's name does mean "fire," the active element of "torch," but the parallels end there. To imagine Loki as a Northern Prometheus carrying fire to the people demonstrates a poor understanding of the Eddas. The god who fills this role in our mythology is actually Heimdall, as told in Rigsthula. He is the bringer of culture, knowledge, and the runes to mankind. As our illuminator, Heimdall is the "torch" that guides the spiritual evolution of our people.

While Loki is an unfit match for Kenaz, he is an ideal one for Kaunaz. Loki represents a sickness among the gods — the spirit of discord, envy, and disease. Whereas Heimdall is the light of progress, Loki is the fire of destruction that tears down what we have built. By bringing about the death of Baldr, he sets the world on a downward spiral ending in Ragnarok, the doom of the gods. It is during this final battle that these two manifestations of fire — creative Heimdall and destructive Loki — kill one another. "Torch" and "ulcer" could thus be thought of as the two sides of a coin — opposing forces that balance each other out.

In relation to other runes, Kenaz is sometimes paired with Isa to represent fire and ice, the opposite poles that meet to create the universe. Perhaps a more insightful parallel exists with Sowilo, the sun. In the seemingly endless winter of the North, the sun is the savior of mankind, the giver of life, and the light of day. A torch, however, represents the sun at night, a sustaining fire to guide us through the darkest time. In an age without electric lights, nighttime changed the entire landscape into a hostile world where malevolent forces roamed freely. Our ancestors' best defense against wolves, witches, and other dwellers of the dark was the torch, a miniature sun that lit up what they knew of the daytime world. Kenaz thus represents Sowilo on an intimate level, an internal sun that keeps us going through the bleakest stretches of our lives.

Kaunaz, sickness, can best be paired with Nauthiz, the need-fire. Our ancestors built one of these fires whenever disease, famine, or any other internal factor threatened the survival of the community. This shared ritual would have been similar to blot, but instead of celebrating the cycle of life the need-fire was intended to heal whatever "ulcer" plagued the group. Nauthiz could be thought of as "turning the corner" on the illness, the stage where the fever breaks and recovery begins. From this point forward, Kaunaz becomes Kenaz — the path to wellness.

In our traditional worldview, the connection between Kenaz and Kaunaz can be considered as heilagr versus oheilagr. The positive use of the torch is heilagr — healthy, whole, and holy. The negative effects of the ulcer are oheilagr — sick, divided, and unholy. Our ancestors saw man as a holistic being, meaning that body and soul are one and there is little separation between the material and spiritual realms. The Kenaz/Kaunaz relationship thus extends far beyond physical ailments. Kaunaz represents addictions, vices, and any other behaviors that afflict one's community. It sets us against ourselves, causes dissension in the garth (see Inguz), and tries to break the bonds of blood and friendship. Kenaz, on the other hand, stands for unity and virtue. It balances us internally and with our environment, mends the fences of the garth, and builds frith with the people in our lives. (For more on Heilagr, garth, and frith, see *Heathen Handbook*, Sec. I.)

Kaunaz can also be looked at in relation to Hagalaz. Just as sickness is a crisis in the life of an individual, the "hail" rune can represent crisis on a large scale such as natural disasters or manmade tragedies. This relationship parallels that of Dagaz and Jera, day and year. Both of these runes symbolize cycles, but Dagaz operates on a smaller, more intimate level than the annual cycle of Jera. Likewise, we face the trials of Kaunaz on a daily basis in our personal lives, whereas Hagalaz rains its difficulties down on the community as a whole.

Today we rarely use actual torches; however, we have all had to rely on a flashlight or candles during power outages or other emergencies. Without these sources of light, we would be lost in a blackened world, stumbling through the darkness, at the mercy of whatever lurks in the shadows. Many people do feel lost — spiritually and emotionally — in the wasteland of contemporary culture. For modern Heathens, Kenaz can thus be seen as a light that leads us back to those things that truly matter in life: family, friends, and folk. It is also the spark of consciousness that both pulls us forward and prevents us from sliding back into a primitive state. According to the lore, Rig (Heimdall) teaches mankind to use the bloodgifts that Odin and his brothers have given us, to rise to our potential, to be predators rather than prey.

Kenaz stands for our teachers, mentors, and heroes who have guided us along to becoming the people we are, but it also stands for our duty to guide the next generation. This rune reminds us of our sacred responsibility to keep the flame burning so that we may pass the torch of our culture on to our descendants.

Kaunaz, on the other hand, symbolizes those things that threaten to break the chain of our heritage and traditions. While plague and famine still occur in the modern world, the more serious sicknesses that afflict our people are mental and spiritual in nature. These ulcers come in many names and forms, but their shared aim is to destroy true diversity by mashing all peoples into a single mold. Monotheism, universalism, and consumerism — all of these viruses have infected our worldview. Kaunaz should serve as a wake-up call to fight whatever opposes our well being.

Gebo

Gebo (gay-boh) gift. Gebo means "gift" in all of our sources. The stave shape of Gebo is one of the "proto-runes" indigenous to Northern Europe and found on rock carvings more than 3,000 years old. It was one of the eight runes dropped from the Scandinavian Younger Futhark as the sounds for "g" and "k" became almost identical in those languages. For example, the ON/OI word for "and" appears as both "*og*" and "*ok*." These sounds remained distinct in Western Europe, though, so the Gebo stave survived in the OE rune-poem. There a gift is described as something that "heartens those that have nothing." In the tongues of ON and OE, the "g" sound is hard, as in "good". It can change in front of vowels, but for modern runic purposes, it will be the hard "g".

Gifting was an essential concept in our ancestral culture, and many examples of it can be found in the lore. There are few sagas that do not contain exchanges of Gebo, and

70

Havamal has no less than nine stanzas that deal directly with gifting. All these examples are tied to the fundamental Heathen ideal of balance and friendship. Odin reminds us that "always a gift looks for a return," (st. 145) and "between givers and those-who-give-back is friendship longest." (st. 41) Simply put, the exchange of Gebo must be a two-way street in order to build the bonds of friendship.

In our traditional worldview, gifting is linked to two concepts that revolve around hospitality, a virtue which can be thought of as generosity in both deed and spirit. The first is the idea that part of the giver's wyrd and maegan are tied up in the gift, so the receiver gets more than just the object that is handed over. This is important for two reasons. First, you have to be careful who you accept a gift from, because your wyrd (the force of your past deeds bearing on the present moment) mixes with theirs. Second, if you receive a piece of the giver's maegan (spiritual strength of power of will), then you are obliged to repay in kind. In this context, the actual gift is not the issue; it truly is the thought that counts. Wealth and knowledge have no intrinsic value outside of what they acquire through the act of sharing them with friends. These gifts carry a value that cannot be measured in dollars, for they are vessels of your maegan. Likewise, if you do not respond to Gebo with a meaningful gift, you have in effect robbed the giver of the maegan you received.

The second idea tied to Gebo is that the stingy man has no friends. This is not to say we must buy our friends; rather, it means that one who does not exchange gift for gift, and thus wyrd for wyrd and maegan for maegan, has not bonded himself to others and cannot feel frith among those who should be his people. Our people have always believed that we should share with our friends and those we respect enough to want as friends. (For a more detailed discussion of wyrd, maegan, and other concepts central to our worldview, see *Heathen Handbook*, Sec. II).

Gebo is not just the act of giving or receiving, it is a cultural norm built around the idea of sharing at every level. True friends do not only share bounty, they also share hardship, grief, and sacrifice. Gathering together for a shared meal and expressions of love and solidarity is just as important for funerals as it is for weddings. Joining a kinsman in giving up a Saturday for an important project is a strong expression of Gebo, and the shared accomplishment that follows the sacrifice will strengthen the community. The crossed lines that form the Gebo stave symbolize the bond, like two people standing arm-in-arm, that is forged between those who support one another within the community.

Gebo holds special relationships to two runes. The first is Wunjo, joy. Few things bring a smile to one's face like a gift. The *Havamal* advises that if you really trust a friend, "blend your thoughts with his, exchange gifts, and fare to find him often." (st. 44) As was said above, each time Gebo is exchanged, the bonds of friendship strengthen. Eventually, neither of you keeps track of who has given what or how often. The Gebo flows freely, as the other person's well-being becomes synonymous with your own. This is frith, the peace and joy of being at home among your people. At this point you have built a garth, an enclosure around the relationship that defines the other person as a friend and ally.

This brings us to Inguz, the second rune related to Gebo. The frith that is created through giving is the bond that creates community, but Gebo is essential to community on an even more fundamental level because the first step on the road to trust is an exchange of respect. This first exchange is followed by others that bring people closer together — gifts of trust and dependability — until community is formed. This garth is represented by Inguz and is the ultimate goal of Gebo. Because most gifts today are symbols of conspicuous consumption, they lack the significance that Gebo had in our ancestors' world. Too often gifts are given out of a sense of social obligation rather than from a desire to share Wunjo and build Inguz with another person. In our self-absorbed culture of individual isolation, perhaps the most valuable gift one can give is their time.

In the Eddas we find examples of Odin giving his eye and Tyr sacrificing his hand to the cause of staving off Ragnarok, but the Gebo of Thor is less obvious. Whenever the gods are at sumble, Thor's chair is empty — not because he does not love drinking with his friends, but because he has dedicated his time to slaying giants and making the world safe for mankind. What gift could be more sacred? Our own efforts do not have to be as heroic as slaying giants to be effective, nor do they have to separate us from kith or kin. Give back to the earth by organizing a group to clean up a local landmark, recycling, or conserving resources. Spearhead a fundraiser for a good local cause. Start a community garden. Get your kith and kin together on a regular basis to build the bonds of friendship. Do those things that need to be done but no one else will do. In these ways, and many others, we can make Gebo an active force in our lives.

Wunjo

Wunjo (woon-yoh) joy. Wunjo can be traced to a root meaning "joy" or "wonder." Some scholars have attempted to tie this rune instead to the *winjo*, "pasture," but there is no evidence to support such a claim. Joy, at any rate, was essential enough to our ancestors' worldview to merit its own rune, and it would be a necessary concept in a system of divination. Like Gebo, Wunjo was dropped when the futharks of Scandinavia shrank to sixteen runes. The "W" sound (double U) gave way to the single "U" of Uruz in the North c. 800 CE. The "W" continued to be used in Western Europe and appears in the OE rune-poem, which describes him who enjoys Wunjo as "blessed with gain and plenty."

An examination of the lore reveals plenty of examples of joy and happiness. The Vanir in general, and Freyja in particular, tend to be associated with laughter, happiness, and lust for life. There is also an entire class of poems called "flytings" that were the ancient equivalent of a "roast" with humorous or even scandalous insults flying back and forth. The Eddic poem *Lokasenna*, where Loki trades crude insults with the other gods, is an excellent example of this type. Some scholars dismiss Lokasenna as a late writing intended to disparage the gods, but their argument is based in a Christian worldview that assumes a deity to be too far-removed from mankind to make an obscene remark, let alone tell a fart joke. Certainly Yahweh lacks any sense of humor as he pouts by himself on a distant cloud, but our own gods and goddesses find no shame in pleasure and, like us, prefer the joy of drinking with friends to the malaise of solitude. This same joyful outlook is present in many of the sagas. Humor, especially in the face of hardship or danger, was highly regarded . The Jomsvikings, for instance, were famous not only for their valor but also for their ability to joke and laugh at certain death.

Another aspect of Wunjo is spiritual wonder or awe. This goes beyond happiness to the pride and humility that overtakes us when standing before the majesty of our ancestors or the ecstasy of a parent holding their newborn baby for the first time. The capacity to experience this positive upwelling of emotion can be thought of as the gift of Odin's brother, Ve, whose name means sacred or holy. Just as Odin gives us Ansuz, Ve gives us Wunjo, the ability to stand awe-struck before the inexplicable or to be filled with joy when we feel the presence of the gods. Heathens can reach toward the divine without feelings of guilt or inadequacy because we share with the gods a love for this world, our people, and ourselves. These two aspects of Wunjo weave together the two sides of frith — the joy of being loved and accepted among our people, and the peace within ourselves to embrace our humanity and face life with courage and laughter.

In connection with other runes, Wunjo holds close ties to Gebo, discussed above, as well as a few others. The first is Mannaz, man. In *Havamal* st. 47, Har (Odin) describes how he traveled alone in his younger years, yet "I thought myself fortunate when I found another; man is the joy of man." This stanza appears in the midst of a lengthy discussion on friendship. The word "man" in ON applies to all genders, and what Odin means is simply that human beings are social creatures. From the day of our birth we are not designed to be alone, and in the hostile climate of our ancestors' world, isolated individuals seldom survived for long. Those who did live alone were usually outlaws, people whose deeds had pushed them outside the garth of society, condemned to eke out a lonely existence separated from kith and kin. Although contemporary culture romanticizes the "lone wolf," this idea is alien to our traditional worldview. Our ancestors understood that joy comes from shared experiences, and the same holds true for us today.

Another line in the OE rune-poem describes Wunjo as "content in a strong community," a clear connection to the rune Othala, our heritage. As said above, joy comes from interactions with others (Mannaz). This joy strengthens the bonds of frith that define us as a people (Othala). Wunjo is the glue that binds a community together.

While there are those who claim to be "solo practitioners," an experience of our way that comes only through books or the internet misses the point. Reading about our ancestral traditions is necessary to understand who we are and where we come from, but to put that knowledge into practice, to advance it from a mental exercise into a physical force, requires being active in a community. Only when we are able to feel the Wunjo that arises from spending time with kith and kindred do we get a glimpse of what it means to truly be Heathen.

Today we tend to think of joy as a temporary emotion rather than an approach to life. This is largely because, regardless of our religion, we live in a Judeo-Christian culture and have been imprinted with that worldview. Wunjo is impossible where people attach guilt to every pleasure or feel only fear and shame when confronted with the divine. These negative emotions have wormed their way into our spirit after a thousand years of domination by the desert god, but they can only drag us down if we refuse to embrace the joy of life.

To break free of this negative influence requires a constant effort on our part to reclaim the Wunjo of our forebears. Our ancestors' positive embrace of life is what Nietzsche calls "saying 'Yes' to the world," a direct reflection of their system of morals that equates happiness with the good, noble, powerful, beautiful, and beloved of the gods. In modern Heathenry, we call this system the Nine Noble Virtues. These virtues are active principles that guide our deeds and stand in contrast to the static "Thou shalt nots" of the Ten Commandments. Simply put, Wunjo is created by living with honor among our folk.

The joy of frith comes from spending time with friends and family and choosing to do what is best for them. Frith is the highest goal of Heathenry. To find it, Heathens must embrace the Wunjo of their life and the world while relishing the happiness and contentment that is only found among the folk. Wunjo happens when we break free from the frozen "I" and move toward the dynamic "we" of community.

Hagalaz

Hagalaz (ha-ga-laz) hail. Hagalaz is known as "hail" in all the rune-poems which describe it as the "coldest" and "whitest of grains." Although the Old English poem tries to give it a positive spin by saying it "turns to water," hail was undoubtedly a destructive element to our ancestors. As a damager of homes and destroyer of crops, hail is a weapon of the forces of chaos that oppose the gods. This comes across well in the OE poem *The Seafarer*: hail fell on the frost-bound earth, coldest of grains. In some later futharks the symbol of Hagalaz changed to a single stave with two crossing diagonals, a shape that suggests a snowflake or grain of hail.

Hagalaz makes at least one obvious appearance in our lore. In the *Saga of the Jomsvikings*, Jarl Haken summons his disir, Irpa and Thorgerda, to rain hail into the eyes of the invading vikings. Although considered ogresses from the perspective of the invaders, disir are the female ancestral spirits of one's family (see *Heathen Handbook*, Sec. VI). Here, these household goddesses use actual hail as a barrier to the viking force, but Hagalaz can be thought of as any obstacle or ordeal that one must overcome to fulfill an oath or achieve a goal.

The Saga of the Jomsvikings presents Hagalaz as a weapon, and this is critical to understanding how it fits into the pattern of the futhark and our ancestral tradition. In its negative aspect, Hagalaz is the active force of chaos and destruction; it is the agent of ruin, as opposed to an idea or state of being. Winter is the enemy; the hailstorm is the weapon.

Another way to look at Hagalaz is as the natural occurrence of crisis, the stimulus for change. In this sense, Hagalaz marks the beginning of any evolutionary process, whether that process is individual maturity or cultural progress. This type of chaos is not evil; it is part of the natural process of growth and change.

Many crises in our history and mythology signal impending change. Joseph Campbell, an iconic scholar of mythology, describes crisis as the moment of truth when actors in the mythic drama realize that the status quo is gone and something must change. Odin experiences such a moment before he and his brothers attack Ymir, as does every hero who answers the call to adventure and takes up his quest. Historically, the coming of the Huns signaled a time of crisis for the Goths because their old world had been crushed beneath the Hunnish cavalry. The Gothic people had to choose between slavery to the Huns or launching the tribes into migration towards a new destiny. Hagalaz destroys the status quo and forces decision. On a personal level, Hagalaz marks the moments when we must move forward or degenerate. The child who does not embrace adulthood cannot really remain a child because the child dies in the hailstorms of physical change. The choice forced by Hagalaz is whether or not we move into adulthood with purpose and confidence.

In relation to other runes, Hagalaz can be related to those closest to it in the futhark order. We discussed Wunjo above as symbolizing the spirit of community and the ties that bind our folk together. Hagalaz represents the forces that try to break those bonds, the trials that test our friendships to see which are true. We have all had "fair weather friends," those who come around when times are good to share in our joy and prosperity, yet disappear just as quickly when the going gets rough. It is during these times of "hail" that we need friends the most. The crisis of Hagalaz thus separates the true from the fake, our real friends who exchange Gebo and bring Wunjo to our lives from those who are merely leeches.

The rune following Hagalaz is Nauthiz, the need-fire. When our ancestors faced persistent "hail" in their community, whether sickness, famine, or any other crisis, they would put out their hearth fires and come together to start a new fire in the ancient manner (see Nauthiz). The idea was likely that the need-fire would counteract the "hail," thus bringing an end to disease, hunger, etc. Nauthiz represents the answer to Hagalaz, the action we take to deal with a crisis.

Hagalaz also has a connection to Isa, ice. Obviously hail is ice, only in an active state (falling from the sky). Likewise, Hagalaz can be seen as being in the midst of a crisis, whereas Isa is the aftermath. For example, the onset of the "Little Ice Age" in the 14th century made some settlements no longer habitable to our people, such as those in Greenland. The shrinking of the land that had been their home was the crisis; the desolate sheet of ice left behind was the result (Isa). Another example is the long and often bloody battles our ancestors fought against the spread of Christianity across Europe (Hagalaz). Today, the physical fighting is over, but we are still coping with the spiritual fallout from adopting a foreign faith (Isa).

Hagalaz can also be related to both Jera and Dagaz in that these runes represent cycles both great and small. Hagalaz is the stimulus that keeps the cycles moving and promotes constant evolution. The experience of Hagalaz is unpleasant, but without it, the impetus for growth is gone and stagnation follows.

In modern times, hail remains a destructive force, although technology has lessened its impact. For most of us, a hailstorm might result in damage to our car's paint job, which is a far cry from the life-or-death situation our ancestors faced by having their crops wiped out or livestock killed. We do face crises in many other forms though.

Whenever our traditional values are assaulted by the forces of universalism that despise true diversity, we are dealing with Hagalaz. When we struggle with self-centered addictions that tear family and folk apart, hail has come to our lives. Hagalaz is every crisis we must overcome as Heathens in a world that would like to see our traditional ways forgotten. Hagalaz is also present as we grow as individuals and as a people. Each challenge and crisis is both a confrontation with ruin and an opportunity to become stronger. Iron is forged in the terrible crisis of fire and hammer, and so too are we hardened and tempered by each trial we face.

Nauthiz

Nauthiz (nou-theez) need. Nauthiz can be traced back to PIE *nau*, "need, necessity, distress, death." The rune-poems say it "leaves one little choice," "constricts the heart," and "is a hard condition to suffer." The implication is that this rune was invoked when one had run out of other options. As Heathens, self-reliance is one of our noble virtues, but it is also true that the gods help those who help themselves. In *Havamal*, Odin advises "it is better unasked, than over-sacrificed for," which is similar to a parent telling a child "don't bother me unless it's an emergency." However, once we have done all that we can and the distress remains, Nauthiz serves as an emergency call for outside assistance.

Nauthiz is one of the few runestaves specifically named in the *Poetic Edda*. In the *Lay of Sigrdrifa*, the valkyrie is teaching Sigurd runes (magic charms) to help him on his quest. One of these is a defense against poisoned ale wherein she instructs the hero to carve staves into the drinking horn and "mark your nail with Nauð" (Nauthiz). Poisoning someone's drink was a common method in our lore for women to take vengeance on men who had wronged them, and Sigurd's half-brother Sinfjotli is killed in precisely this manner. An attempt is also made on the life of Egil Skallagrimsson this way, but he uses his rune-knowledge to shatter the horn so that the tainted mead drains to the floor.

The idea of Nauthiz as a counter to dire situations occurs in other poems of the Edda. The first rune spell Odin lists in *Runatal* (see APPENDIX II) likely included carving Nauthiz, as he says, "it will help you/ with sickness and sorrow/ and the whole of affliction. " A similar concept is found in *Baldrs Draumar* when Odin, grief-stricken over his son's impending death, calls forth the seeress from her grave. While he surely uses his twelfth rune spell (*Hav.* 157) to make the dead woman speak, the poetry describes her three times as "need-bound" by Odin. Much like carving the stave on a fingernail allows one to overcome the effects of a poisoned drink, Nauthiz here gives Val-Father a measure of control over the seeress, forcing her to answer his summons. These examples offer insight into the compelling nature of this stave and how our ancestors used it.

In relation to other runes, Nauthiz is best understood by its ties to those closest to it. Hagalaz represents a crisis that afflicts the community, and Isa is the lingering consequences of the crisis. This destructive situation causes a "need" for relief, healing, and assistance. Nauthiz is thus an entreaty to the gods for help.

Often this was done by means of a need-fire ceremony. To execute this ritual, all the hearth fires of the homes in a community were extinguished. A new fire would then be ignited in the ancient manner. The shape of the Nauthiz stave itself suggests this ritual where two sticks were "crossed." One had a string tied to both ends, and the slack was wrapped around the other so the "rubbing" made a rotary motion. The end was inserted into a hole with kindling, and the friction ignited the flame. This points to a sexual connotation of Nauthiz, which is appropriate considering the sexual aspects of the fire festivals of May Eve (Beltane) that marked the coming of summer. Once the need-fire was burning, each family would light a torch from it and carry it home to rekindle their hearth fire.

Fire itself is and has always been a symbol of culture and progress for our people. Our ability to control fire holds a direct relationship to how far our civilization has come, from the first man to have a fire burning in his cave to our ability to harness the sun's rays for energy. On the other hand, an out-of-control fire forces us to take a step backward. By extinguishing the old hearth fire, our ancestors symbolically "put out" whatever ailed the community. The new flame that was brought in from the need-fire would bring new luck and help guide our way forward again (Kenaz). This ritual was done at least once a year at a seasonal blot, usually to mark the start of summer, but it could be performed at any time during the year if they perceived the need was great enough.

Although much has changed since our ancestors' days, human needs remain the same: food, shelter, love, acceptance. While our forbears' struggles centered around the material necessities of life, they at least had the support of kith and kin to rely on no matter how bad things got. They knew where they belonged and what their role was in the community. Simply put, their lives had meaning. Love and acceptance were a given even if food and shelter were not always guaranteed.

Today that situation has been reversed. Seldom are we concerned with having a roof over our head or where our next meal will come from. Even if disease or drought wipe out crops and livestock across the region, the local store will still have groceries. The necessities we lack instead are of an emotional nature. The breakdown of the community, and ultimately of the family, has left us a society of individuals, "unique" yet anonymous faces lost in a city of people just like us.

Our ancestors would not have grasped the idea of an existential crisis, but in a culture where our only purpose is to consume, it is no wonder that we are left searching for meaning. When we light the need-fire today, it is seldom to pray for rain, calm seas, or an end to winter. Our Nauthiz is for reawakening, to rekindle the frith found in faith and family. Our need is to be true folk once again.

This leaves modern Heathens with a two-fold relationship toward Nauthiz. The first allows us to use this rune as a constant measuring stick to help us understand necessity. Modern society has a hard time distinguishing between need and want, but confusing the two is unacceptable for Heathens because distraction from necessity will only take us further down the path of the destruction of our people and culture. Keeping our eye on Nauthiz will remind us of what is necessary for our people to reclaim our ways and reap the frith that follows.

The need-fire provides the other aspect of our relationship with Nauthiz. When our ancestors performed this ritual, the idea was an active resistance to whatever threatened their community. The ritual itself may appear to be a pointless superstition to modern eyes, but the key element is being active. The crises of Hagalaz and the negative consequences of Isa will not sort themselves out if we passively endure. It is up to us to step forward and ignite the fire of positive change. Nauthiz thus stands as a symbol not just of necessity but of action.

Isa

Isa (ee-sa) ice. Isa means ice in all the sources. Like Hagalaz, Isa is connected to chaotic natural forces. The rune-poems speak of ice in relation to travel, as it made journeys over land more difficult and sea voyages impossible. Thus the time to go a-viking — to travel, trade, war, and raid — was limited to summer. Once winter came on and ice began to spread over the north, outdoor activities came to a sudden halt.

The OE rune-poem describes Isa as "cold and slippery," yet "fair to behold," both a danger and a beauty. The ON adds that "the blind need to be led across," both warning that you must be in possession of your senses to challenge this rune.

Isa plays a crucial role in our lore. In the *Prose Edda*, Snorri tells us the icy realm of Niflheim mixes with the heat of Muspell to create the first being, Ymir. Later Audhumbla, the primordial cow (see Fehu), licked Buri, the first god, from out of the ice. Just as it requires both male and female to create a child, our mythology expresses this same duality: passive ice combined with active heat or friction (Audhumbla's tongue) to bring forth life. The same forces work to destroy life at Ragnarok, the end of this age. Unlike the biblical apocalypse, however, Ragnarok only marks the end of a cycle, just as winter marks the end of a year and gives way to spring.

In the millennia that pass between creation and destruction, the static Isa is depicted as the Aesir's most active enemy. Living in the far north, our ancestors developed myths that depicted their battles against frost-giants (cold weather) and dread of the Fimbulvetr, an ice age where winter never ceases. Had our people settled in warmer climes farther south, like the Indo-Europeans who spread into India, Persia, Greece, and Rome, our myths would have reflected different threats to the folk. On the balmy shores of the Mediterranean, for example, ice is no great challenge to survival, but Isa would still represent whatever forces of chaos oppose us.

Isa can be related to several other runes. Above, Hagalaz was discussed as a crisis, the active form of ice, like being in the midst of a tornado or other emergency. Isa, on the other hand, is the path of destruction left behind by the storm. A vivid example from literature can be found in Kurt Vonnegut's *Slaughterhouse 5*, a novel centered around the fire-bombing of Dresden in World War II. The main character lives through the actual bombing (Hagalaz), but afterwards the once thriving city he knew now resembles the surface of the moon. Majestic buildings have been replaced by smoldering craters. The "hail" has passed, but the survivors now drift among the remains of a dead landscape. To our ancestors, the aftermath of such a crisis had no better symbol than a sheet of ice.

Isa can also be thought of as a static situation, one that has been "frozen in time," so to speak. Such a conservative stance holds a certain appeal to Heathens as we struggle to carry on our ancestral worldview. This role is exemplified amongst the gods by Tyr, the defender of law, order, and tradition. As such, Isa both stands in opposition to and works in tandem with the dynamic force of Jera. Jera is movement, the Odinic wind of change that blows through the folksoul and urges us beyond our comfort zone. Isa helps us to stay true to our ways, to remember, to be proud. Jera pushes us to evolve, to invent, to explore. The key to the relationship between Isa and Jera, Tyr and Odin, is to find the balance. Isa connects us to the past and gives us a sense of who we are; Jera carries us into the future and provides an image of what we can become. (For more on this topic, see Odin and Tyr in *Heathen Handbook*, Sec. IV.)

If we view the crisis of Hagalaz as the stimulus to change and the need-fire of Nauthiz as our response to that stimulus, then Isa and Jera are the two possible outcomes: Isa is stagnation; Jera is growth. The key to facing change successfully, or even realizing that you have failed to do so and are stuck in Isa, is to understand that ice thaws and breaks. The ice that covered the world of our ancestors was driven back each spring to reveal new life. Isa can always be overcome.

Isa plays a subtle yet crucial role in the lives of modern Heathens. Our fallout comes not from the onset of winter or other physical phenomena; rather, the aftermath we must cope with is the spiritual baggage of a foreign faith. Many of the problems Western civilization faces arise from Indo-European descendants trying to reconcile our innate values with a Judeo-Christian worldview, which is like forcing a square peg into a round hole. Our traditional virtues of strength, pride, and self-reliance can only clash with alien

88

ideals of meekness, humility, and "giving it all to god." Carl Jung, Nietzsche, and other great minds have pointed to these irreconcilable differences as the source of our neuroses and the sickness underlying society as a whole. After a thousand years of being frozen in a false tradition, we are tasked with melting through the ice that binds us to an unnatural belief system. Isa thus represents our biggest challenge — to reject what is "normal" in favor of what is natural, to break the mental fetters that deny our identity and potential, and to view the world as a gift to be embraced as hale, whole, and holy.

This ice will not break itself. The enemies of Isa are initiative and action; its allies are found in pessimism and apathy. To break the stagnation of Isa in ourselves and our people we must face up to the crisis, take the necessary action, and smash through the frozen stillness of decay to reach the dynamic harvest of growth and frith.

Jera

Jera (yeer-ah) harvest. Jera is referred to as "harvest time" in all the rune-poems, which also associate it with plenty, abundance, and fruitfulness. Later it came to mean "year," the annual cycle of the seasons, but it has always been especially tied to late summer/fall when "the Earth gifts us her bright fruits." Even though agriculture naturally comes to mind when we think of a harvest, the concept applies equally as well to tending herds of cattle, sheep, etc. For ages before our ancestors settled down to farm they survived by hunting; thus the idea of Jera may have originally been tied to the bounty of the hunt or the natural increase from breeding livestock.

Jera can be found in many places in our lore. The sagas mention a "harvest man," a land wight who held sway over the fertility of the fields. During sumble, toasts were drunk to Njord and Frey "for good harvests and for peace," which points to the association of the Vanir with this rune. While this is true, the Aesir also play their part during this crucial time of year.

Just as the aid of the earth goddess was needed to sow the seeds, grow the grain, and gather the harvest, the sky god was required to make it rain. Almost all of our northern deities have a connection to fertility, but it is Thor, the Thunderer, who bolts across the sky leading the storm clouds behind him. The rain itself is symbolic of the *heiros gamos*, the sacred marriage between the heavens and the earth. Our mythology expresses this as the marriage of Thor and Sif, whose golden hair represents the ripened grain. Their sexual union promises fertility to the fields and a fruitful future to the folk; conversely, if they fail to unite, sterility and death come to the land. As a way to honor the god and goddess and encourage the seeds to grow, people would have ritual sex in the fields during planting season. This holy act — aside from being enjoyable — would help ensure a bountiful crop at harvest time.

Jera holds relationships with several other runes. As the only "broken" runestave, Jera suggests movement. It is formed of two interlocking Kenaz staves joined in sacred marriage, much like the sexual activity of Thor and Sif. Just like their union produces the harvest that promises our future prosperity, Kenaz is the "torch" that guides us there. Without the coming together of the earth goddess and the sky god, the Kenaz staves turn away from each other and the "sickness" of Kaunaz is brought into the land. Without Jera, Kaunaz would bring drought and disease, and our ancestors would turn to the need-fire (Nauthiz) to reconcile the relationship of earth and sky.

Jera is also connected to Dagaz. As "year," Jera stands for the cycle of the seasons: spring, summer, fall, winter. Dagaz, "day," represents the same cycle in a smaller scale: morning, noon, evening, and night. This also applies to the cycle of life. Jera symbolizes birth, life, death, and rebirth on a grand scale, from the creation of Midgard, our life in it, to its destruction at Ragnarok, and to the new world that follows. Dagaz operates on an individual level, taking us through our personal Ragnaroks and rebounds as we mature over the course of our lives.

Whereas the previous rune in the futhark, Isa, represents the static and unchanging, Jera is dynamic and evolving. Likewise, the "ice" of winter forebodes darkness and death, but the summer "harvest" brings hope of light and life. We also related Isa to the preservation of tradition as a role of Tyr. Here, Jera can be seen as the force of change by which Odin prods us forward, the drive that led our ancestors across the seas to new lands just as it takes us beyond our planet to explore the universe. The balance between these runes is the key to who we are as Heathens: Isa holds us solidly in our identity; Jera pushes us toward our destiny.

Jera can also be related to Raidho and Wunjo. If we consider the idea of a harvest as a gathering in of the fruits of our labor and the joy and satisfaction that follows, the relationship is clear. Any task, regardless of whether it is physical or spiritual, is a journey of work and perseverance. Each half of the broken Jera stave might represent a sickle or plowshare, symbols of the sweat involved in a harvest of any sort. The joy of Wunjo is the "why" of our harvest. Pride and satisfaction offer strong motivation to complete whatever tasks we face and bring the benefits home to our people.

In this post-modern era, our existence does not hinge on the local harvest. Too little of what we eat comes from our own backyards, and a crop failure in one area only means that we will pay a higher price for that item at the store. Even though few people are involved in large-scale agriculture, Jera still plays an active role in our lives.

On an obvious level, we all labor — physically, mentally, or both — at our profession. That harvest comes in the form of paychecks, promotions, and a sense of pride in a job well done. Additionally, we should all have goals that we strive to meet, and accomplishing them constitutes another harvest. But more than that, Jera represents our ability to think ahead, to make plans, to delay gratification today in order to reap bigger rewards down the road. Often this requires setting aside our own desires in favor of the needs of family and folk. No harvest could be more important than building a brighter tomorrow for future generations, and for that dream to grow into reality demands that we get busy sowing the seeds today.

Jera is, at its core, a result or an effect. In this sense, it stems from our actions. To gather in the joy of a stronger family and folk, we must do all the work that stands in between us and our desired result. That work never ends, just as a farmer's work is never done, for to stop is to give in to stagnation and decay. Jera is continual motion; it is the eternal labor of going forward.

Eihwaz

Eihwaz (eye-whaz) yew. Eihwaz means "yew tree" and is referred to as such in all the rune-poems. It shares the same etymology as the Anglo-Saxon rune Yr, "bow made of yew," and the Icelandic poem calls Eihwaz a "taut bow." Across much of Europe yew was the wood of choice for bows because of its strength, flexibility , and durability — even the 6,000 year old Iceman ("Otzi") found in the Italian Alps was carrying a yew bow at the time of his death. In England, yew was also the most common material for magic wands (ON *gandr*).

   Eihwaz is one of the "proto-runes" found on northern European rock carvings dating back thousands of years, and the stave itself has no equivalent in other writing systems. In runic inscriptions Eihwaz seldom appears, but when it does it is usually in association with magic. Phonetically, Eihwaz represents a vowel sound between long "e" and "i" as in "either" (ee-ther or eye-ther), but it can also be a short "i. "

In our lore Eihwaz can be associated with the bow god, Ullr, but it is most often tied to the World-Tree, Yggdrasil. Even though this tree is called an ash in *Voluspa*, the references to it elsewhere in the Eddas more accurately describe a yew. The key to understanding the World-Tree is to imagine it as the central pillar that connects our world to all the others — the realms of the dead, the gods, giants, elves, and so forth. The yew may have provided this same access. In late summer the yew emits a toxic vapor, the inhaling of which may trigger shamanic-type visions. Thus a person could conceivably sit under a yew, breathe deeply, and enter an altered state wherein they "travel" the nine worlds. It should go without saying that this method of altering consciousness is dangerous. Folk tales often depict witches as dwelling beneath the yew, which served to warn people away from experiencing a "bad trip."

The yew has long been a symbol of life and death in Celtic and Germanic tradition. The roots of the tree are believed to bind the dead in the grave to prevent them from coming back and haunting the living. In pagan times, people were either buried in yew groves or else the tree was planted at grave sites. This custom passed on into Christian England, as churches were built on or adjacent to the groves so the dead would be buried in a yew-filled churchyard. Up until the 1700s a yew bough was still placed in the grave. On the continent, a German custom held that children conceived in their family's yew cemetery would soak in the spirits of their ancestors.

Eihwaz has connections to several other runes. Just as it symbolizes the World-Tree, Ansuz can be seen as Odin, especially in his aspect as a traveler on the tree. Ansuz is the shaman, the magic man who gains knowledge through altered states of consciousness. Eihwaz is the actual territory he explores, the hidden lands that exist just behind the veil of waking consciousness. Carl Jung called this territory the collective unconscious, which is the storehouse of all human memories. It is the home of the ancestors below and the gods above, places that communicate to us through our dreams.

If Ansuz is the shaman and Eihwaz his *terra incognita*, the vehicle by which he travels is Ehwaz, the horse. For Odin , the obvious association here is with Sleipnir, his eight-legged horse, but he has other vehicles as well — a pair of ravens and two wolves. Each type of animal can be seen as a different state of consciousness. The wolves are the berserker frenzy, the unleashing of one's inner dogs of war to strike fear in the heart of the enemy and make one impervious to their weapons.

Whereas the wolves represent letting go of control, the ravens are an exercise in pure concentration. They symbolize Odin's ability to extend his consciousness outside his body, a practice known today as "remote viewing" or "astral travel." The ravens carry the mind across the physical plane and into the heavens, but they cannot penetrate the underworld; only the death-horse Sleipnir can take its rider to the halls of the ancestors. Each of these animals allow access to different Eihwaz states. They also represent the psychoactive substances that enable one to enter them. Dozens of such substances occur naturally in Northern Europe, but investigating which plants correspond to which vehicles falls beyond the scope of this book.

Having established the traveler, the vehicle, and the territory, all that remains is the trip itself, Raidho. "Riding" is the journey, the actions you take to reach your goal. Often this involves ritual. It may be as elaborate as Odin's ordeal on Yggdrasil or as simple as sex in the yew cemetery; either way, these are deliberate actions taken to achieve a specific purpose. Another example is the rite of *utiseta* — spending the night "sitting out" on a burial mound to communicate with a dead ancestor. All these facets of "riding" evoke Eihwaz states of consciousness.

In this era of science and technology, we rarely take magic, myth, or ritual seriously. The problem is that, regardless of our beliefs (or lack thereof), we look back on our traditional ways through the lens of the contemporary society we live in. This modern worldview equates myth with falsehood, ritual with play-acting, and magic with illusion, which is far from how our forebears saw these things.

Myths are stories designed to help us grasp our place in the world and our role in it. Ritual binds us together as a community and guides us through the transitions in life from birth to death. Magic is how we influence the world around us according to our will. All of these factors work together to give us purpose and a sense of who we are. It is our current lack of these things — meaning and identity — that lies at the base of our neuroses and the malaise underlying our culture.

The World Tree is an evergreen. Our ancestors believed that the life force of the trees that shed their leaves flowed into the evergreens to be preserved through the winter. The same could be said for our heritage. The core of our culture has been preserved for us; it only waits for spring to come forth again. Eihwaz can be seen as the repository of our traditions and as our path to becoming whole and hale as a folk again.

The journey on this path need not be shamanic, but it will alter both our view of the world and how we interact with it. From the roots that connect us to the spirit of our ancestors, to the limbs that reach toward our gods and the future of our people, Eihwaz provides a basis for modern myth and ritual that can guide us into the future.

Perthro

Perthro (per-throw) gaming. Perthro has puzzled the scholars who have attempted to discover its origin and meaning. It can be traced to the PIE root *per*, "to try, to risk." This definition is reflected in the OE rune-poem which refers to Perthro with the terms *"plega"* and *"wlancum"* which meant a kind of competitive striving and high-spiritedness. It also shares a linguistic link to gaming via the Persian *ferz*, which is a gaming piece. Linguists have noted that an initial "P" sound is rare in Germanic languages, thus the creator of the futhark may have borrowed this rune-name from Celtic or another nearby tongue. Regardless of whether it is indigenous or not, the Germanic tribes were no strangers to the concept Perthro represents. Historians such as Tacitus have written about their taste for gambling, an activity they took rather seriously.

Instances of gaming occur often in our lore. *Voluspa* tells of the gods playing tafl, a game similar to chess, in the Golden Age following the creation of Midgard. In the days after Ragnarok, the surviving gods again discover the gilded gaming pieces, a poetic way of saying that they "pick up the pieces" of their culture and establish a new order. *Rigsthula* mentions that the sons of Jarl, the representatives of the highest class, compete in athletic events like swimming as well as at board games. *Grettir's Saga* and *Egil's Saga* both mention competitions of wrestling and rock lifting. While all classes had to be in shape just to do the work necessary for survival, the aristocracy also needed to stay mentally sharp in order to lead their people.

In an age where books and literacy were uncommon, gaming provided an outlet to engage the mind, match wits with a competitor, and learn to think ahead. Tafl and other games are mentioned in many sagas, and one gets the impression that they served as a means of practicing one's skills at home before they were tested in the larger, more lethal arena outside of one's garth.

Perthro can also be tied to the Norns, the forces of fate (wyrd) that influence one's life. When we gamble, we take for granted that there is an element of chance that affects the outcome. Our traditional worldview also understands this, although with one major difference. "Chance" is not some random event; it is determined by one's past deeds as they are shaped by present events. This equation is symbolized by the three Norns: Urd is what has already been done; Verdandi, what is being done now or "becoming;" and Skuld is the "debt" that we owe. Far from being arbitrary, chance to a Heathen is the result of past and present actions. As is often said, "we are our deeds." This is similar to the idea of karma in that it teaches all actions have consequences that we are responsible for — good, bad, or otherwise.

Perthro holds close ties to the runes nearest to it. As a time of testing, Perthro calls to mind Odin's ordeal on the World-Tree (Eihwaz). Initiation poses a real risk. In effect, Odin bets his life that he can endure nine nights on the tree, a gamble he both wins and loses. He dies to the person he once was, naive and unknowing, and is reborn a changed man, stronger and wiser, with knowledge of worlds beyond this one. He risks a second initiation in the Well of Wyrd at the root of Yggdrasil by sacrificing his eye, which is called "Father of the Slain's wager." Exploring the uncharted domains of Eihwaz constitutes a gamble on one's self, a trying of one's wyrd to determine if one's dues have been paid.

Following Perthro comes Algiz, the "life rune." It has been used to represent our entrance into this world at birth and, when upside down, our exit from it at death. Perthro stands for everything that happens in between. Life itself is a test, a time of trial, a game. And while our tombstones seldom convey more than dates of birth and death, it is our daily struggle with adversity — and the actions we take to overcome it — that define who we are. Perthro may symbolize our doom, our destiny, but more importantly it represents how we fight in the face of fate.

Perthro is especially pertinent to contemporary Heathens. Like Raidho and Gebo, this rune is a verb, an action. Even though gaming is just as much a part of our culture now as it was for our ancestors, merely watching football on TV misses the point. Perthro demands participation. As average life expectancy continues to rise, staying both physically and mentally active becomes more and more important. Studies have shown that games like crossword puzzles and sudoku help prevent dementia as we age, and regular exercise battles everything from heart disease to depression. Simply stated, active gaming improves the quality of our lives.

Much the same could be said of gambling. When our ancestors placed a wager, they knew their wyrd weighed on the result. Again, putting a hundred bucks on who will win the Super Bowl is irrelevant (unless you happen to be playing in it). Perthro only comes into play when we bet on ourselves. The outcome then becomes a direct reflection of our past actions (practice and preparation) as they meet present conditions (our mindset, energy level, and desire to win) that determine our destiny.

This highlights the difference between two kinds of luck: the kind that refers to blind chance in which we have no active role, and the kind of luck that comes from our wyrd. The key is locus of control. Winning a wager on another person's skill is blind chance, but it is different if we are competing. Practice trains us to make good decisions when we are hurt, tired, or angry. Competition ignites the fire that drives us toward victory. These are the factors that will determine if we win or lose, and these factors are within our control.

When we externalize these things and compete vicariously through others, we surrender that control. Such a surrender makes us much more likely to externalize control over a myriad of other facets of our lives, such as where we spend our money, how we think, or what we believe. Choosing to compete on our own merits and internalize the heart of our luck makes us more likely to retain control in other areas of our lives. Perthro thus serves as a reminder that what we do today has consequences tomorrow. For good or ill, the future is in our hands.

Algiz

Algiz (al-geez) protection, elk. Algiz (sometimes called Elhaz) can be traced back to the PIE root *el*, which can mean "elk, elm, alder, or elder." In the rune-poems it appears only in the OE where it is called *eolhx*, "elk sedge" — a type of water reed that "burns with blood those who would lay hands upon it." The OE word *eolh* means "elk," which can be derived from the Germanic root *alhiz*, "elk" or *algiz*, "protection, defense." Scholars find the latter a more probable origin, and it would offer a more likely choice for a system of divination than "elk." "Defense" also fits the idea of elk sedge as a plant that "grimly wounds" anything that touches it. Algiz is unique among the futhark in that it does not represent an initial sound; rather, it stands for the final "-z" found in numerous Proto-Germanic words (such as many of the rune-names). When Proto-Germanic evolved into ON, the final "-z" became a final "-R" {a more buzzed sound than the "r" of Raidho) as in ThorR or FreyR.

Algiz can be found in several places in our lore. As "elk" it connects nearest to Eikthyrnir, the hart that stands atop Valhalla along with the goat Heidrun. These creatures eat the leaves of Yggdrasil, from which they produce two essential fluids — Heidrun's milk becomes the mead of inspiration, and the liquid that drops from Eikthyrnir's horns fills the Well of Wyrd from which all rivers have their source. Eikthyrnir translates as "Tree-Thorn," a name that indicates this animal defends the World-Tree from the forces of chaos.

The OE rune-poem's attribution of this rune to "elk sedge" also points in a revealing direction. Though it has lost this meaning over time, "elk" was an archaic word among our people for swans or geese. Because elk sedge grass grows in swampy areas like marshes or fens, it was more likely named after these water-dwelling birds than for the large deer that prefer the camouflage of the woods. Our ancestral tongues had smaller vocabularies than the hodgepodge that is modern English, so individual words tended to encompass broad ideas rather than specific objects. The idea expressed by "elk" was of something grand. Just as what we now think of as elk are the grandest of deer, our ancestors recognized swans and geese as the grandest, most graceful of birds.

This particular aspect of Algiz ties it to the swan maidens – women who, with the aid of special cloaks, could shape-shift into swans. Like Freya's falcon-coat, these cloaks helped induce an altered state of consciousness that facilitated out-of-body experiences (see Eihwaz). Mircea Eliade, an expert on shamanism, says of such items that "the very structure of the costume seeks to imitate as faithfully as possible the shape of a bird." He further notes that the concept of "flight by the aid of bird's feathers" is common in pre-Christian indigenous cultures like that of our ancestors.

Our lore speaks of both men and women using animal forms, though men more often wore bear-shirts (ON *berserkr*) or wolf pelts to channel the ferocity of these beasts in battle. The purpose of the swan-coat was to allow the mind to travel through water and air. *Volundrkvida* describes how the sons of Ivalde meet three ladies beside a lake: "Maidens flew from the south into the the Myrkwood.../ Nearby the women lay their swan-shapes." They stay with the brothers until the ninth winter when they must fly away again, "their orlog to try."

Swan maidens appear also in *Helreid Brynhild*, and their existence is known beyond the *Poetic Edda*. In other Indo-European lore, they play a role in the Celtic tale of Oengus mac Oc as well as in the Vedic tradition of protecting swan maidens known as *gnas*, procreators, and *apsaras*, water goddesses.

As "protection," Algiz occurs in many magical incantations in the Eddas. Seven of the eighteen rune-spells that Odin describes at the end of *Havamal* serve protective or defensive purposes. These range from dulling the edges of enemies' weapons to protecting princes to quieting the waves of the sea. Likewise, some of the charms that Sigrdrifa and Groa teach to their young initiates are intended specifically to keep them from harm.

No figure in our lore better embodies the spirit of protection than the All-Mother Frigga. In the quest to save Baldr, she scours the earth, extracting oaths from every living thing not to harm her son. The natural inclination to shield one's children from pain and anguish suggests an inherent tie between Algiz and mothers in general, yet other evidence points to an even deeper connection to Frigga. The name of her hall, Fensalir (Marsh-hall), specifies its location on low-lying and often flooded land that is an ideal habitat for elk sedge and water birds. Archaic names for some of these birds refer either to Frigga or the mistletoe that avoided swearing her pledge of protection for Baldr. The idea of tying the mother goddess and her role as protector to water birds is not limited to Germanic lore. In ancient Rome, the temple of Juno on the Capitoline Hill kept sacred geese in the temple precinct. These geese were famous for warning the Romans of a night attack by the Gauls during the siege of 390 BCE.

Algiz also appears on archaeological artifacts. The Lindholm amulet features an inscription of 24 runes, three in a row of which are Algiz. Adjacent to them are three Tiwaz runes, which most scholars agree are meant to grant victory to the wearer of the amulet. It only makes sense that the trio of Algiz is intended to insure that person's protection.

This rune occurs as well on Northern European gravestones as the "life rune" to indicate one's date of birth. Some authors compare the shape of this rune to a person standing with their arms raised in a "V" for victory, though there is no indication that our ancestors saw it that way. More likely, this stave represented the footprint of Frigga's messenger – the white "elk" welcoming a newborn into life. The appearance of such a bird outside the home would have been a good omen indicating a healthy birth and good wyrd. This idea has been passed down to us as the tradition of a stork "delivering" babies. It also acts as a balance to the black birds of Odin that arrive when death is imminent and usher the souls from this life. The upside-down Algiz or "death-rune" carved beside the date of one's passing would thus mark the talons of a raven or crow.

Algiz can be connected to several other runes. As a magic charm, it can provide protection for one's home

(Othala) and personal property (Fehu) from destructive natural forces (Thurisaz) or other crises (Hagalaz). It is still used as a "hex sign" on the houses and barns of the Pennsylvania Dutch here in Vinland as well as in Europe. Algiz also works in tandem with Raidho as a protective measure for journeys away from home.

Looking deeper, Algiz shares a connection to Laguz, water. In addition to the waters that support and defend Frigga's hall, those that drip from the antlers of Eikthyrnir flow through the Well of Wyrd and back up through the World-Tree. This cycle represents how our past actions continue to shape who we are and the people we will become.

There are valuable lessons to be learned from the elk we know today. When a herd stands together, they can hold their enemies off indefinitely. So it is with modern Heathens. Alone, we are vulnerable to the claws of a decadent culture and its empty materialism; as a community, our protective antlers can interlock to form a shield wall in our defense, much like the stag horn that Frey wields at Ragnarok.

Sowilo

Sowilo (soh-wee-loh) sun. Sowilo means "sun" in all our sources. It appears in all the rune-poems, which refer to it as "the light of the world," "a shining radiance," and a guide to sailors. Many scholars believe sun-worship to be the most ancient Indo-European religion, dating back several thousand years into the prehistoric era. Numerous depictions of circles and swastikas from those times testify to the importance of the sun in the early spiritual expression of our people. While the symbol of this rune most often appears as three strokes (as above), examples have been found with up to a dozen, making it look like a connected series of Kenaz runes stacked vertically on top of one another.

Sowilo is common in our lore. *Voluspa* says "the sun shone from the south" when Odin and his brothers shaped Midgard from the corpse of Ymir, "then was the grassy plain, growing with green leeks." This ties Sowilo to the

108

fertility function of the elves and Vanir as producers of life and the natural world. Yet Sowilo is also essential to the Aesir in their role of creating and maintaining order. The sun serves as the first time-keeping device, which the gods use "to count that time by years." Apart from merely numbering the days, the sun separates the nighttime world of magic and mayhem from the orderly daytime realm of man. Grimm tells us the rising sun chases spirits back into the underworld, and Snorri describes a sure sign of Ragnarok occurring when the wolf Skoll swallows the sun, thus plunging the world into darkness and chaos.

Another interesting aspect of the sun in our lore is that it appears as both a male and female. *Voluspa* speaks of the goddess Sunna who "knew not what quarter of the sky held her hall." Snorri echoes this by naming the driver of the sun-chariot as Sol, daughter of Mundilfaeri. While most cultures imagine the sun as a strong, masculine deity, the softer touch of solar rays in the far north may be the reason our ancestors so often viewed her as a life-giving goddess. However, other Eddic lays paint a different picture. *Sigrdrifumal* refers to the sun as "the shining god," a fierce warrior who wields the sky as a shield. We associate this god with Odin's son, Baldr, who Snorri says is "so bright that light shines from him." Like the sun itself, Baldr is "born" at winter solstice, symbolic of the sun's struggle against cold and chaos, and "dies" at summer solstice, the point at which the solar orbit begins to decline from its annual peak.

Sowilo has close relationships to other runes. The first is with Ehwaz, the horse. About half the times that the Eddas mention the sun, it is in association with Arvak and Alsvinn, the horses that pull the sun-chariot. Ancient artifacts have been discovered that also highlight this connection. The Bronze-age sun-wagon found in

Trundholm (Sweden) has led at least one scholar to speculate that Ehwaz may symbolize the sun's path through the heavens, which suggests Sowilo and Ehwaz, sun and horse, might have been tightly linked in the oldest runic system. Although that relationship grew more obscure as centuries passed, the sun maintained its position as a beneficent deity while the horse remained highly honored.

Sowilo can also be related to Kenaz. Like Jera, the shape of the Sowilo runestave can be seen as multiple Kenaz runes. However, unlike the opposed sides of Jera — summer and winter, light and dark — the Kenaz staves that form Sowilo overlap in an unbroken chain of torches, suggesting Sol Invictus, the sun at the very height of summer. *Havamal* also supports this connection: "Fire is best for the sons of men, and the sight of the sun." Grimm tells us that our ancestors knew the sun as the eye of Wodan (Odin) by which he saw all the events in Midgard. The fiery torch of Kenaz itself allows us to see when we otherwise could not, a mini-sun that repels the darkness and guides us to safety.

Sowilo finds its antithesis in Isa, ice. The Icelandic rune-poem calls Sowilo "the nemesis of ice," and these runes can be easily imagined as polar opposites: hot and cold, day and night, etc. But rather than set Sowilo and Isa against each other, Snorri portrays them as the driving forces of creation: "Just as from Niflheim there arose coldness and all things grim, so what was facing close to Muspell was hot and bright, but Ginnungagap was as mild as a windless sky. And when the rime and the blowing of the warmth met it became the form of a man, and he was called Ymir." One way to interpret this myth is that, while both extremes are necessary for creation, life only exists somewhere in between. Most of us prefer the fun and sun of summer, but to become fully formed human beings requires enduring the dark of winter as well. A Heathen's life should be ruled by neither indulgence nor abstinence but balance. To paraphrase the advice of *Havamal*: eat, drink, and be merry, but don't become an obese drunkard who makes an ass of himself.

For contemporary Heathens it can be difficult to appreciate the depth of meaning that the sun held for our ancestors. In the far north, the seemingly endless months of cold brought up fears of the Fimbulvetr, the Terrible Winter that would last three seasons without seeing the sun. During this prelude to Ragnarok nothing would grow, people would starve, and darkness would rule the land. Imagine then their sense of relief as the days began to lengthen and temperatures warmed. The strengthening of the sun's power was a promise of renewed life to the folk, a sign that the gods had overcome their enemies and better times were ahead.

Few of us today live or die by the sun. Our lack of real ties to the land or the need to be near family means that we live wherever our jobs take us or, if we can afford it, wherever we find the climate comfortable. Even for those who still dwell in harsh northern climes, modern conveniences lessen the physical impact of winter. Does that mean Sowilo has lost its importance to us? Hardly. Above all, this rune is a symbol of hope. After the desolate winter of Isa, Sowilo represents the reawakening of the folk-soul, the return to our roots and celebration of our heritage. Sowilo sheds light on our past, just as it illuminates the road to a brighter tomorrow.

Tiwaz

Tiwaz (tee-waz) Tyr. Tiwaz refers to Tyr (OE Tiu) in all the sources. The OE rune-poem says "it holds true through the night clouds," which some scholars have taken as a reference to either the moon or a constellation. Although the moon is seen as a male deity in our lore, it seems more likely that what the poet had in mind here was the North Star, Polaris, as it is also called "unfailing" and a sign of "confidence to the noble." This rune is often associated with the Irminsul, the world-pillar of ancient Germanic cosmology. The Irminsul filled the same role for our Continental ancestors that the World-Tree, Yggdrasil, did in Scandinavia by serving as the axis mundi — the central column around which the rest of the world rotates. This axis cam be imagined as extending into space and being capped off at the North Star, the point around which the rest of the sky rotates. As the guardian of law, order, and tradition, Tyr would naturally be represented by Polaris, "true north," the one unchanging point in the heavens that people could always rely on to guide their course.

Both Scandinavian rune-poems call Tyr "the one-handed," a reference to the best-known story about him in our lore. Snorri tells us how Loki, the shape-shifting trickster god, birthed monstrous offspring that would become powerful enemies of the gods. They were sent away where they could do the least amount of harm except for the pup Fenris who was kept under watch in Asgard. As Fenris grew into a giant wolf, the Aesir could no longer leave him unbound, but no chains were strong enough to hold him. Finally they had the elves design a magical fetter from impossible materials, but the only way Fenris would agree to let them tie him up with it was if one of them would place their sword hand in his mouth as a pledge. As they had no intention of letting the wolf loose again, the gods knew that whoever volunteered would be sacrificing his ability to fight and his status as a warrior. Despite this steep price, Tyr stepped forward and gave up a part of himself for the good of the community. Thus, describing him as "the one-handed" is not a statement about a physical deficiency but rather about the integrity of his character.

Tyr plays a part in other myths from our lore such as *Hymiskvitha* and *Lokasenna*. In *Sigrdrifmal*, the valkyrie instructs Sigurd to "invoke Tyr twice" to gain victory and carve staves on the hilt of his sword, one of which (if not the only one) is certainly Tiwaz. The fact that a sword, several spear heads, and helmet have all been found that actually do have Tiwaz etched into them underscores the importance of both myth and magic among our ancestors who were skilled in the use of runes. A trio of Tiwaz staves also appear on the Lindholm amulet, and we can only assume that these were likewise intended to bring victory to the wearer.

Tiwaz holds connections to several runes. Like Kenaz, the torch, the North Star serves as a guide through the black of night. While not a source of illumination, Tiwaz instead orients us to our surroundings and allows us to stay true to the path. These runes can be thought of as working in tandem — Kenaz lights the way as Tiwaz directs us to our destination.

Many people relate Tiwaz to Sowilo, both as signs of victory. Above we mentioned Sigrdrifa's invocation to Tyr as a means of insuring victory in combat, and Sowilo may be tied to this concept as Sol Invictus, the Unconquerable or Victorious Sun. Our ancestors viewed sunrise every morning as a triumph over the enemies of gods and men as the bright rays pushed malevolent forces back into their shadowy realms. Most peoples around the globe relate the sun to their preeminent deities, and Heathens are no exception — Odin and his son Baldr can both be seen as sun gods. However, evidence points to a time before the folk-wandering when Tyr reigned as ruler of the Aesir, a position that would have certainly connected his rune to that of the sun.

The transfer of power from Tyr to Odin points to the most interesting and dynamic relationship between Tiwaz and another rune — that of Ansuz. Above we described Tyr as the upholder of law, order, and tradition, a role that preserves our identity as a people and cohesiveness as a community. The sacrifice of his hand to the wolf illustrates these virtues by maintaining the established order (binding Fenris) for as long as possible. Odin, on the other hand, presides over times of tumult, progress, and evolution. Where Tiwaz is the rock-solid foundation which we rely on and return to, Ansuz is the wind of change that pushes us forward into the unknown. Odin's sacrifice of himself reveals a means not to maintain order but to destroy it, to slay Ymir and build a new world from the old corpse. For Heathens it is not a choice between Tiwaz and Ansuz, tradition and progress, but a matter of knowing when to look back to our roots and when to focus ahead.

Tiwaz ranks as more important to the folk today than ever. The example of Tyr reminds us that the noble warrior fights for family and folk, no matter the cost. Embracing this rune in our lives means sacrificing our personal wants and binding our destructive desires for the good of those we love. Our battle may be spiritual and cultural rather than physical, but struggle is struggle, and Tiwaz is a constant reminder of how and why we should fight.

The people of Northern Europe have lived for more than a millennium under the yoke of a foreign faith, and even though the virtue of the ancestors still lives in the descendants, we have forgotten our traditional values. Without our code of honor to guide us, the bedrock of our culture and identity has deteriorated. We have lost our way.

Just as the pole star stands constant in the night, so too can our heritage and tradition provide sure guides. Tiwaz is the guardian of this inheritance, and as such, both the rune and the god stand for permanence in a constantly changing world. No matter how much our surroundings shift, we can always look up and find Polaris, just as we can always look to the ways of our ancestors to orient ourselves as we pursue change or react to it.

Berkano

Berkano (ber-kan-oh) birch. The etymology of Berkano can be traced back to PIE *bherek*, "to shine, bright, white, birch." It is called birch in all of the rune-poems, each of which makes reference to its branches. This may be significant as birch twigs were used in spring festivals to promote the fruitfulness of the coming year. Scholars commonly associate the birch with fertility cults as a symbol of new life and especially the rebirth of nature around the vernal equinox. Berkano in our lore can be tied to any number of goddesses significant to spring such as Ostara, Freyja, and Walburga.

Like Berkano's PIE root, our deities are described as "bright" and "shining," and the goddesses are "white-armed." The white bark of the birch thus makes a natural connection to the inhabitants of Asgard. Additionally, the birch's silver tint calls to mind the love of precious metals exhibited by Freyja and other goddesses, and this may offer another reason that the birch is held in such high esteem.

The birch plays an important role in our lore for more than just its color. Its bark has proved to be the longest lasting of all trees, a property that made it an ideal writing medium for ancient peoples who lacked paper. Among our ancestors, hundreds of messages on birch bark have been discovered in Bergen, Norway. The inscriptions date to medieval times, and are nearly all written in runes, even though Roman (Latin) letters had been in use in Norway for hundreds of years at that point. This may indicate that, while Latin was the alphabet employed by those beholden to the Church, runes remained the writing system of choice for the common folk who held onto this part of our heritage even after Heathenry was outlawed. The content of the Bergen inscriptions covers the spectrum from business letters to magical invocations to dirty jokes, but many are love notes — an appropriate topic to address on the fertile birch.

Compared to other runes, Berkano's most revealing relationship is with Eihwaz, the yew. Just as branches of yew were placed in coffins to either bind the dead or guide them to the underworld, so branches of birch were left in bedrooms in order to encourage successful reproduction. What these two trees may represent are times of transition and the cycle of life — yew for the passage into death and birch for the calling forth of new life. During certain celebrations, young women and men were decked with birth twigs to insure their fertility, and the same was done to livestock. A similar May custom could be found in parts of Britain where a birch limb would be tied over the door of one's desired lover.

Apart from birth and death, spring and fall, the birch and yew may also symbolize altered states of consciousness.

117

Above we related Eihwaz to the shaman's journey into other worlds, particularly the home of the dead. In summertime, the yew emits a toxic vapor that may facilitate the Hel-bound hallucinatory trip. The Berkano experience, however, would lead to a different destination. The bark of the birch itself produces a narcotic effect simply by being chewed, but the more likely source of the trip is the Fly Agaric mushroom commonly found in birch woodlands. Researchers in this field of study have tended to associate the psychedelic mushroom with Freyja, and her "feather cloak" or "falcon form" that allows her to travel to other realms may be a poetic euphemism for use of the Fly Agaric.

Berkano may also hold an ancient connection to Tiwaz. As the original sky god, Tyr represents victory over the forces that oppose us in the many battlefields of life. As a symbol of the earth goddess, Berkano promises food, comfort, and shelter to this and future generations. Standing next to each other in the futhark, Tiwaz and Berkano can thus be seen as the traditional partnership of man and woman, the teamwork and sacrifice necessary to raise a strong family. From another perspective, these runes also symbolize the functions of the Aesir and Vanir — Tiwaz creating order by triumphing over chaos and Berkano bringing about the fruitfulness of mankind, beast, and field.

For Heathens today, Berkano should embody the sacred feminine. As for all pagan peoples, balance should play a key role in our lives, one that includes the relationship between woman and man. Far too often this balance is thrown out of whack by a tendency to overemphasize the "warrior ethic" — a misguided claim that our forefathers were all blood-thirsty Vikings whose hobbies included murder, rape, and pillaging. This is not only a historically biased view based on Christian sources but a gross distortion of what it means to be Heathen. Our ancestors — both men and women — were warriors when they needed to be, but that only reveals a small part of their identities. They were also farmers, weavers, adventurers and providers, mothers, fathers, wives, husbands, and faithful friends. So many of the sagas focus on traditionally male-dominated activities that women seem to get short shrift in our lore. But keep in mind that these were written a couple centuries after the conversion by men who were educated by the Church — an institution with a long history of treating women as second-class citizens.

Recent attempts have been made to shed light on the lives of our foremothers. Excellent examples include Kathleen Herbert's *Peace-Weavers and Shieldmaidens* and Hilda Ellis Davidson's *Roles of the Northern Goddess*. Books like this are a good place to start, but restoring balance to our worldview will require more than just reading. Tacitus describes how the Germanic tribes 2,000 years ago regarded their women with a sense of religious awe, and it is past time for the women of today to reclaim their honored status. For Berkano to be active in our lives now means not only that we must treat women with the respect they deserve but that women must assert their equal position in the partnership.

Ehwaz

Ehwaz (eh-waz) horse. Ehwaz can be traced to the PIE root *ekwo*, "horse." It appears only in the OE rune-poem which says it is "splendid of hooves, where heroes and the wealthy... bandy words." This offers some idea of the esteem in which our ancestors regarded the horse as well as its close connection to nobility. According to Tacitus, the Germanic tribes saw certain horses as sacred and interpreted their sounds and movements as messages from the gods. Among the Celts, the goddess Eponia was herself depicted as a mare, and the sagas describe Norwegian farmers honoring a fertility deity known as Volsi in the form of a horse phallus.

    Ehwaz occurs often in our lore. Snorri relates that the Aesir ride their horses every day to Wyrd's Well to judge the dead. He names each of these steeds but says the best is Odin's horse, Sleipnir. This eight-legged beast is the child of Loki, a character known for delivering monstrous offspring such as the World-Serpent and the Fenris Wolf. Unlike his siblings, however, Sleipnir serves as an asset rather than an enemy to the gods. His eight legs can be seen as a depiction of supernatural speed, but some scholars connect them instead to the four pallbearers that carry the dead to the grave. To this end, the Eddas describe at least two occasions where Sleipnir carries riders down the road to Hel — a deed nowhere attributed to any other vehicle. Skalds also used Sleipnir as a kenning for "ship" because of his ability to cross over boundaries, both natural ones such as bodies of water and otherworldly ones like the threshold between life and death.

Several other horses, like Sigurd's steed Grani, merit multiple mentions in the Eddas, but perhaps the most valued equine legs next to Sleipnir's belong to the celestial pair who pull the sun's chariot. Arvak and Alsvinn are pictured as leading the solar orb across the sky. This relationship between Ehwaz and Sowilo has roots stretching back to Indo-European times (see Sowilo). Snorri describes the sun/horse partnership in terms of metalsmithing: the sun is a "molten particle of smelted iron," while the horses act as a furnace for removing slag from the metal. Although Snorri ties this relationship to the Iron Age, artifacts such as the Trundholm sun-wagon push it back into the Bronze Age. The sun/horse connection likely predates mankind's manipulation of metals.

Ehwaz also has links to other runes. The shamanic complex of Ansuz, Raidho, Eihwaz, and Ehwaz has been explored in the sections on these other staves. To recap, Ansuz represents the traveler into altered states, Raidho the trip itself, and Eihwaz the *terra incognita*. Ehwaz, then, is the vehicle that facilitates the journey. In the section on Berkano we looked into that rune's possible connection to the Fly Agaric mushroom as Freyja's "falcon form," her

121

vehicle for reaching altered states. Other gods may be associated with other vehicles, such as Frey's ship Skidbladnir that can carry all the Aesir yet is small enough to "fit in one's pocket," and his boar Gullinbursti that moves "across sea and sky." Odin possesses more means of travel than anyone else (see Ansuz), including the mysterious mead of inspiration, Odroerir. As with any other vehicle, we can only speculate as to the specific ingredients of this mead, but the rich variety of psychoactive herbs and other substances found in northern Europe leaves no shortage of Ehwaz vehicles for every deity to possess their own unique means of travel.

A connection also exists between Ehwaz and Othala, one's ancestral lands and family property. For Indo-European folk, the horse has long been a symbol of sovereignty and control of territory. This may originate in an era when disputes over land were resolved by letting one's horse roam over it. The area the horse traversed would constitute one's claim. J.P. Mallory suggests that Hengist and Horsa, the founders of England, may have adopted their names as ritual titles in their quest to claim part of Britain for their confederation of Germanic tribes. Much like the Vanic rite of blessing or claiming land where the deity circled the area in a wagon, an annual horseback ride around the garth (see Inguz) would have renewed the boundaries of one's property. The use of a slain horse's head on a *nidstang* ("insult-pole") to curse the land, as done in Egil's Saga, may have been seen as a counteraction to the blessing rite, a means of chasing well-meaning wights away from an enemy's garth.

It is difficult for us to conceive how crucial our ancestors' relationship to their horse was to their welfare. Havamal advises that "no man should be ashamed" of his horse, just as none should be embarrassed by their family or friends. A person's horse was at times so dear to them that they would be buried together to travel the road to Hel or Valhalla. Today we might think of Ehwaz as a valued car, truck, boat, etc. Although we may spend lots of time and money on such vehicles, few of us would consider taking them to our grave. Our deep affection for our modes of transportation ultimately falls far short of the ancient bond between man and horse.

As in our ancestors' days, the modern world offers a wide array of options for entering altered states. What we lack, however, is the right mindset for the journey. Our culture regards the use of psychedelics as not only wrong but criminal. Although these substances can be dangerous and should always be approached with caution, they were part of our traditional experience of divinity. The problem now is that we no longer have a spiritual context for their use. A thorough reading of the Eddas will show that the gods were not recreational indulgers; when their vehicles were used it was to achieve a definite purpose. This intention makes all the difference. The proper use of Ehwaz vehicles is as a means to an end; taking these substances as an end in itself is merely drug abuse. Ehwaz affords a way to reconnect, but this journey is best not taken until we can approach it with sincerity, sanctity, and responsibility.

Mannaz

Mannaz (man-az) man. Mannaz means "man," which in Indo-European languages can refer to a person of either gender as well as the whole of the human race. It can be traced back to PIE *mannusos*, "man," and holds that meaning in all the rune-poems. All three poems allude to our mortality, saying we are the "waxing of dust" and that "our frail bodies" will be returned to the earth. As we have seen with other runes, this seems to be a Christian overlay onto an older Heathen concept. Images of man being created from dust and returning to dust are biblical ones originating in the sands of Middle Eastern deserts; nowhere in Northern lore do our ancestors speak of being made of dirt. The Heathen idea of death stands in sharp contrast to this, as our lives have been described as a vivid tapestry woven by the Norns and ending when our threads are cut. A Heathen death, then, marks the climax of a valued work, a monument to one's deeds rather than an escape from one's sufferings.

Mannaz looms large in the lore. While our myths tend to focus on the actions of the gods, the events they depict only make sense and take meaning in the mind of mankind. Man has always been the great storyteller; for as long as we have had the ability to speak we have been spinning tales to help us understand the world and our relationship to it. Regardless of the divine nature of mythology and the uncanny characters it portrays, it is, by far, about mankind.

The most significant reference to the race of man in the Eddas occurs in *Voluspa*. As part of our creation myth, the seeress describes how Odin, Hoenir, and Lodur find two pieces of driftwood called Ask and Embla. These names are usually translated as "Ash" and "Elm," but the poetic nature of Old Norse allows that a specific tree name may refer to any tree in general. At any rate, the wooden beings are "of little maegan… without orlog," until the gods bestow gifts on them: "breath gave Odin, mind gave Hoenir, blood gave Lodur, and good color." In effect the gods infused their blood into the veins of mankind, raising us from dead wood to living beings that are tied into the Web of Wyrd.

Our creation myth offers a marked contrast to the biblical account. Adam and Eve are also "orlogless" (do not know death) in the Garden of Eden until they eat from a certain tree that makes them like their gods (Elohim). But unlike the Aesir's gifts to man, the powers Adam and Eve gain must be stolen when the Elohim are not looking; what follows is not a blessing but a curse on humanity.

In *Voluspa*, man ascends to the level of the gods and is forever bound to them by partaking in their spiritual essence. In *Genesis*, man is "fallen," cast away from the sight of deity by the stain of "original sin." This fundamental difference in the relationship of man and the gods in our ancestral mythos versus that of Judaeo-Christianity underlies the opposition in these worldviews. Heathens do not seek nor require redemption for "falling short of the glory of god," rather, we seek to live up to the virtues of our deities to prove worthy of the gifts they have entrusted to us.

Mannaz has ties to several runes. The OE rune-poem says "we are each other's merriment," a sentiment echoed in the Icelandic poem's statement that "man is the joy of man." The latter is a direct quote from the *Havamal* that illustrates the bond between Mannaz and Wunjo (see Wunjo).

Earlier we discussed how Odin, Hoenir, and Lodur gifted mankind with a piece of themselves, thus imbuing us with a godlike nature (Ansuz). This divine spark of the Aesir makes us unique among other animals with our abilities to speak, to abstract, and to create. Yet Ansuz accounts for only around 2% of our DNA — the fraction that separates us from our nearest simian relatives. The remaining 98% is Uruz, our animal nature that includes our instincts and will to survive. Uruz rules our subconscious, the murky area beneath our waking thoughts from which our drives and desires arise. Ansuz hovers over Uruz like a watchful eye keeping our passions in check. Caught in the middle of these warring factions is Mannaz, our conscious mind. This stave represents everything that defines us as human — the balancing factor between abstinence and indulgence, thought and action, god and beast.

Another key to unlocking Mannaz can be found in its relationship with Ehwaz. The very shape of the Mannaz stave suggests the two legs of a rider atop the horse of Ehwaz, and this image of horse and rider may hint at the rune's meaning. On one hand, the relationship between man and horse serves as a mark of our ancestors' identity.

The immense value of the horse in commerce, agriculture, and war gave them the strength to thrive and spread, a strength that has defined who we are. On the other hand, the partnership of man and horse is also a metaphor for our relationship with nature. Any rider who abuses, neglects, or coerces their horse will pay the price for it down the line, as will any person or culture that mistreats the natural world. But if a rider seeks the deep emotional connection that is possible with a horse, the result is a spiritual bond. By approaching all of nature in this positive way, we can expect the same results.

If we look at the Mannaz stave as a symbol of man on the horse, an obvious question comes to mind. Where are we going? For our ancestors, a whole world lay unexplored before them, a challenge they welcomed with a curious mind and a stout heart. This drive to set foot on new lands was not only about expanding the external boundaries of Midgard, it was about testing their internal limits to discover what manner of men they were, then pushing past that to become better. Joseph Campbell calls this "the hero's journey," and it is precisely the type of quest found in our myths. The problem we face today is that mythology has lost its meaning, and our personal hero's journey seems to have little purpose. Too often we seek our fame in material goods rather than noble deeds. Having failed to challenge ourselves, we are left sitting in a pile of empty possessions wondering what it all means. Mannaz thus stands as the ideal for a Heathen life, a call to get on our horse and experience the world. This rune reminds us that it is not enough to merely exist; to be worthy of the gods' bloodgift we must brave the ordeal, surpass our limits, and aspire to something more.

Laguz

Laguz (la-gooz) water. Laguz means "water" in all the
sources. It derives from PIE *lakus*, "body of water, sea,
lake." Bodies of water filled two symbolic functions in the
minds of our ancestors. In one sense they served as
boundary markers. The OE rune-poem says "Water to land-
folk seems never-ending when they set sail," an apt
description of the vastness of the ocean. Although the
Vikings were widely known as skilled seafarers, their
vessels were designed for speed rather than safety, and
whenever they could they stayed within sight of the
shoreline rather than risk the open ocean. The Eddas depict
Midgard as surrounded by an immense ocean that is bound
by the world-serpent at the edges of the earth.

Water thus separates the home of mankind from "no
man's land," the realm of giants. Smaller bodies of water
like rivers also served as natural dividing lines, such as the
Rhine was between the Germanic tribes and Rome. Islands

128

encircled by lakes or rivers were seen as places outside the law, as the boundaries of one's garth extended only to the water's edge. The ON word for a duel, *holmgang*, means "island-going," as crossing the water took one outside the garth to a place where disputes could be settled without threatening the balance of the law in one's community.

The other traditional function of water is as a sacred site. Tacitus says the goddess Nerthus lived on an island in a lake, and springs and wells were often named for deities who were thought to dwell in or near them. Visitors to such sites sought healing or blessings of fertility. In Scotland these places are especially tied to groups of three or nine maidens, a connection also found in the Eddas. *Voluspa* describes the three Norns as dwelling at Wyrd's Well at the base of the World-Tree. It is here that they "set down laws" and "the fates of men." The water in Wyrd's Well represents the deeds of mankind which are absorbed by the roots of Yggdrasil. This water cycles up through the branches and falls back into the well as drops of dew, thus affecting the flow of present and future events (see *Heathen Handbook*, Sec. II).

Another well plays a key role in our lore — that of Mimir. It also sits under a root of Yggdrasil, but unlike that of the Norns, Mimir's Well holds Odroerir, the mead of inspiration. This well is thus the source of wisdom, the runes, poetry, and magic. In *Havamal*, Odin describes his first drink from Mimir's Well as a defining moment in his life, after which he began to "be well-informed, to grow and thrive as well." Mimir allows Odin this drink after his self-sacrifice on the World-Tree and also teaches him nine runes ("mighty songs"). Later Odin sacrifices his eye in the well for a second drink that enables him "to carve some himself" — in other words, to create nine more runes. Presumably, these two draughts of Odroerir result in the eighteen magic charms that Odin lists at the end of the *Havamal*.

Apart from those named above, Laguz has a special relationship to at least one other deity. Said to be the son of nine sisters, Heimdall was born from the waves of the sea itself. The nine maidens who bore him may be connected to the nine Scottish wells and again to the Norns, who at times appear in the Sagas in groups of nine. Such a tie to Wyrd's Well would suggest Heimdall is the lifeblood of Eihwaz, tying us to all the realms of existence. For its part, Eihwaz immerses us in the water of Wyrd so that all we do has meaning and consequence.

As for Mimir's Well, the Laguz therein is the source of Ansuz, inspiration. Ideas do not just pop into our heads from out of nowhere. Carl Jung teaches that they emerge from the waters of the subconscious mind — the home of our gods and ancestors. When Odin drinks of Odroerir, in effect he dives into the memories of all who came before him, thus gaining the wisdom of the past to guide his present actions and shape the future.

The gods of our folk have never stopped speaking to us, but over centuries of neglect their voices are but a whisper. Today we are learning to turn off the external noise of pop culture and tune into our heritage once again. Laguz represents our return to the Well, the inner voice that calls us back to the troth of our ancestors. Being Heathen in the modern world demands dedication to the study of history, but reading the lore can only take us so far. At some point we must trust in our intuition to dip into the subconscious waters of Laguz. It is by drinking in the wisdom of the past that we, like Odin, "discover the runes" — the secrets to a better way forward.

Inguz

Inguz (ing-ooz) Frey. Inguz (sometimes called Ingwaz) means "the god Ing," a deity connected to the Danish people in *Beowulf* as well as to the Ingaevones that Tacitus lists as one of the three original Germanic tribes. Of these three tribes we are told only that they are named after the sons of Mannus (Mannaz) and that the Ingaevones are "closest to the sea" (Laguz), which may point to an underlying link between this trio of runes. Like Kenaz, Inguz was initially a half-size stave in the Elder Futhark, although later futharks extended it to full size by either lengthening the lines past the top and bottom of the lozenge as in the OE futhorc or, in Scandinavia, adding a vertical stave. As with Thurisaz, there is no one letter in English comparable to the phonetic value of Inguz. Its sound is a nasal "ng" as in "riding" or "gifting. "

Inguz appears only in the OE rune-poem, which relates that the great god Ing was "first seen by the East Danes"

131

and "later eastward over the waves departed," and "a wagon ran after." The mention of a "wagon" ties Ing to the Vanir, and this vehicle may be Frey's famous ship Skidbladnir. That this deity is one and the same as Frey is evidenced by the Scandinavian title Ingvi-Frey or Ing-Fro. The term "Frey" itself is not a name but an honorific that means "lord" (just as "Freyja" means "lady" in the proper sense). "Ing" can be traced to ME *enge, ynge* and ON *eng, engi*, which all mean "meadow." "Ing-Fro," then, is the "Meadow-Lord," a deity of fertility connected to the animals and fields inside one's garth or odal lands. The shape of the Inguz stave suggests the enclosure or boundary around the garth, and thus can be seen as the fence that separates one family's "meadow" (land) from their neighbors'. Property rights have always been a mark of Indo-European peoples, and the sagas record blood-feuds that began over something as simple as one person grazing their sheep on another's land.

Inguz is one of the "proto-runes" found on rock carvings in Northern Europe that are thousands of years old, yet it also appears on pregnant goddess figurines from pre-Indo-European times (before 4500-2500 BCE) as a symbol of a sown field. In Inguz, then, we have a stave tied to agriculture from its earliest stages in the North that, with the spread of our Indo-European ancestors to the region, came to represent the sanctity of ownership that remains a cornerstone of our culture.

As we would expect from such an essential concept, Inguz has left a heavy imprint on our lore. In *Ynglinga Saga*, Snorri says that Frey married the giantess Gerd, and their son Fjolnir was the progenitor of the line of Norwegian kings known as the Ynglings (descendants of Ing). *Skirnismal* in the *Poetic Edda* describes how Frey and Gerd got together with the help of Frey's trusted friend Skirnir.

Some have seen in this myth a depiction of the annual sowing of the fields wherein Frey, the Meadow-Lord, unites with Gerd, the "soil" of the garth, to bring forth a fruitful harvest. As with most ancient myths though, this tale has multiple layers of meaning.

On one level it is about man and the gods taming the giantess earth, which is to say we began to plow and plant crops rather than just gathering wild grain. On another level, it is a piece of the Ragnarok puzzle that underlies nearly all of Norse mythology. *Skirnismal* reveals how Frey gives up his magic sword as part of the bride-price for Gerd, thus surrendering this mighty weapon to the enemies of the gods and leaving himself to fight with only a stag's horn at the final battle. The Swedish scholar Viktor Rydberg makes a convincing argument that Frey's sword is the same "sword of vengeance" crafted by Volund to cut down the Aesir. This weapon changes hands several times, and it is the result of a love-sickness rune that causes Frey to relinquish it to the giants. Whether or not you agree with Rydberg's assessment, *Lokasenna* makes it clear that Loki mocks Frey for giving up such a valuable weapon.

In relation to other runes, Inguz holds close associations to Kenaz and Nauthiz. Across Northern Europe, our ancestors would carry torches on an annual trek around their land to mark the borders of their garth. There are a few ideas wrapped up in this ritual that may not be obvious to us today. One is that, as we will discuss in the section on Dagaz, the world of man only exists as such in the light of day. The artificial boundaries we draw on Midgard disappear when the sun sets — order retreats into the house by the fireside, and chaos has free reign over the darkened land. By walking the edges of their property with a torch — a miniature sun — our ancestors established that inside those borders they were the force of order to be reckoned with.

While stones and fences marked boundaries to one's physical neighbors, carrying the torch served the same purpose for supernatural ones such as wights. Another concept tied to this ritual has to do with its timing. Just as the need-fire ceremony would be performed at the coming of spring (see Nauthiz), so too would this rite of land-claiming. The idea was that the near absence of the sun over the dark winter months would have weakened or erased the boundaries of the garth, thus retracing them with the fresh flame of the need-fire delineated one's land for the duration of the next cycle. The Inguz rune can be seen as two Kenaz staves facing one another and connected at top and bottom, thus these torches outline the garth just as walking the perimeter would.

Few of us today own a meadow, raise crops, or breed livestock. Any land-claiming ritual would be a short affair in the city or suburbs, yet the concept of garth remains just as relevant to us now as it was in pagan times. Garth is more than the land one lives on; it applies also to our personal relationships. This can best be thought of in terms of concentric circles. The innermost circle is one's family, the people you trust with your life and well-being without a doubt. The next circle is your extended family, then close friends, associates, and so on. (See *Heathen Handbook*, Sec. II, for more on the subject.)

Such garths are not maintained by carrying a torch around them; rather, we renew these bonds just as Odin recommends in *Havamal*: by spending time with the people in our garth, going to see them often, and exchanging gifts. Ing-Fro is the bringer of frith to the garth, and his rune is active in our lives to the extent that we build peace and prosperity inside our circles. Inguz teaches us that "good ences make good neighbors," but more importantly it reminds us to stay ever-vigilant in securing the safety and happiness of those nearest and dearest to us.

Dagaz

Dagaz (tha-gaz or da-gaz) day. Dagaz means "day" in all our sources. It appears only in the OE rune-poem which calls it the "messenger" and "light" that "grants ecstasy, good hope, and a boon to all." This gives some sense of the joy and relief with which our ancestors greeted the sunrise each morning.

On some early inscriptions Dagaz comes after Othala as the final stave of the futhark, but the consensus among most researchers places it in the penultimate position. It should also be noted that, while modern authors usually present Dagaz as a "d" sound, it is rarely used as such in ON. Generally its sound is a hard "th" as in "then." It is sometimes transliterated into English as "dh" (as in "Odhinn") and can be thought of as the "dth" sound in "width" as opposed to the softer "th" of "with." In ON/Icelandic, Dagaz became the letter eth, ð.

Dagaz is another "proto-rune," as it can be found in Europe as far back as the fifth millennium BCE in some areas. This marks it as part of a pre-Indo-European culture that Marija Gimbutas calls "Old Europe." This culture is attached to the spread of agriculture across Europe, where it replaced hunter-gatherer societies. The Old Europeans were matrifocal (centered around the feminine principal and goddess worship) and allegedly did not practice war. Gimbutas claims that for these peoples, the Dagaz stave represented the butterfly — a symbol of fertility and the goddess. When the very war-like Indo-European tribes overran the earlier culture, the same sign came to represent the double-headed axe — a symbol of the thunder god (Thor, Donar, Perkunas, etc.). His axe (or hammer) is the lightning that illuminates the stormy sky, threatening the night with the power of day and smashing the dark giants. Although the theory of Old Europe remains controversial, it provides an interesting context for the evolution of the Dagaz stave from a precious butterfly to the vicious hammer of Thor.

Dagaz first appears in our lore as a means of time-keeping, which is to say a method of creating order. *Voluspa* tells of Odin and his brothers creating Midgard from the corpse of Ymir, yet still "the stars knew not their place." It is not until the gods "went to their judgement seats" (held a Thing, or law-meeting) that "morning twas called, and middle day,midforenoon and evening, to count the time by years." Are we to imagine that before this time the sun, moon, stars, and planets drifted randomly through the cosmos? Of course not. What the seeress here describes is an era before mankind developed a mental framework to organize his world.

The origin of order is the observation of patterns in our environment. Stars are given names and placed in constellations, and their movements across the sky serve as a calendar to predict the changing seasons as well as to record the myths of our folk. Mankind thus gains a measure of control over the "gaping void," and from this humble beginning he comes to master his world.

Just as chaos precedes order in the scheme of creation, so our ancestors marked the start of each day at nightfall. Night is thus seen as the mother of Day, and the year also begins with the darkness of winter. For the Celts this occurred on Samhain (the night of October 31st through the morning of November 1st) and for the Germanic peoples on the Twelfth Night of Yule (the night of December 31st through the morning of January 1st.) Beyond dividing time, Dagaz also separates the orderly world of light, life, and men from the chaotic one of darkness, death, and giants. The boundaries of the garth (Inguz) exist only in the light of day. Once the sun sets, the whole of Midgard (Middle-Garth) is given over to the enemies of gods and men — ravenous wolves, evil sorcery, and ill-working wights. As Saxo records, "night was the time to fight with monsters, but day the time with men."

In conjunction with other runes, Dagaz can hardly stand apart from Sowilo, as day is nothing more than the time we are blessed with Sunna's light. Just as Sowilo represents hope, so Dagaz represents the fulfillment of that hope: security, prosperity, and a bright future. In the section on Sowilo we discussed how sun-worship is likely the most ancient Indo-European religious expression, and it is therefore not surprising that the Dagaz stave is found next to sunwheels and other solar symbols on Northern European rock art dating back thousands of years. If we relate this rune to Thor's hammer, the lightning strike, it plays a similar role to Kenaz, the torch, as a source of light in darkness. Both serve to defend order in times of chaos,

138

out the torch symbolizes man's control of fire, whereas Mjollnir is the explosion of the thunder god's weapon.

Dagaz is also closely tied to Jera. The cycles of day and year form the two basic units of time. From these arise both history and science, as mankind uses them to begin measuring the world and making rational observations based thereon. While day and year both represent the cycle of birth, growth, death, and rebirth, Jera addresses it on a grand stage — the changing of seasons, the planting and harvesting of crops, the coming of war or peace — all events that impact the community as a whole. Dagaz, on the other hand, operates on a smaller and more personal scale: rites of passage, working toward individual goals, and dealing with the trials, joys, and disappointments that life throws at us.

In our modern world of cities that never sleep, neon lights, and street lamps on every corner, it is difficult to comprehend just how dark and dreadful night could be in our ancestors' day. We catch a glimpse of it during power outages or when watching horror movies (the action of which always takes place in the dark). But in an age before Thor's lightning was harnessed to power our homes, the terrors of night were very real. The European black wolf stands chest-high on the average adult and can weigh 200 lbs. One would easily tear a man apart, and packs were known to attack houses in winter as other prey grew scarce. Day, then, was a reprieve from the danger of enemies lurking outside the door. More than that, Dagaz represented man's turn to go on the offensive, to reclaim the territory that had been trespassed in the night.

Today, this rune acts as a symbol of the reawakening, of returning to our roots and laying claim to our spiritual heritage after a thousand years of night. We stand at the dawn of this new day; Sunna's rays are only just peeking over the horizon. With a long road yet ahead of us, Dagaz promises we will once again have our place in the sun.

Othala

Othala (oh-tha-la) Inherited property. Othala means "odal lands," those that belonged to a family as a whole and could not be sold or traded. This property was passed down from one generation to the next and included the family home and burial mounds. Othala appears only in the OE rune-poem, which says, "Homeland is cherished be every man... at his dwelling in constant prosperity." This strikes a similar chord to our modern aphorism, "Home is where the heart is," except that in earlier times this rune was rooted in a particular place — the land that held the graves of our ancestors.

Although a few of the oldest inscriptions of the Elder Futhark show this stave as occurring immediately before Dagaz, the majority of the evidence places Othala in the final position. The concept of Othala is implicit throughout our lore. In its worldview, Heathenry is inherently tied to the lands in which we have our roots, specifically those of

141

northern and western Europe where our ancestors staked their claim and forged their identity. Inseparable from this is the idea of property ownership that serves as a cornerstone of Indo-European civilization.

It was through the possession of Othala that people acquired a say in their government, a place in their community, and a vested interest in defending it; a man without land was one without loyalty to or standing in his society. As Heimdall (Rig) implores his son Lord in *Rigsthula*, "get ancestral property, a long-established settlement." Only after Lord fights for land and wins it is he proven worthy of his name and divine parentage. Naturally, not every man was capable of conquering large territories, but every man was expected to be the master of his own domain. As Odin advises in *Havamal*, "home is better though it be small, it is a man's own house."

Later in *Havamal*, another stanza relates that "a man should not be ashamed," of any of his property. This is a reference to both the ancestral inheritance of Othala and the movable or "liquid" wealth of Fehu as standing guard against the lean times of Nauthiz. The relationship between Othala and Fehu can be found in writings that span the centuries from medieval to modern times. A typical example from our lore occurs in *Hrolf Kraki's Saga* where the brothers Helgi and Hroar "took the kingdom, including all of King Frodi's wealth, his lands (Othala) and his movable property (Fehu)." Moving from the 13th century sagas to Chaucer's *Canterbury Tales* of the late 14th, a line from "The Miller's Tale" shows how "the town parson planned to make her his heir, both of his movable property and of his house." Othala and Fehu appear again in the works of 18th century French philosopher Jean-Jacques Rousseau, who observes that prior to the use of money, wealth "could scarce consist in anything but lands and cattle, the only real goods which men can possess." It is fitting that the same runes mark the start and close of the Elder Futhark, as we began our journey with the wealth of the individual and end it now with that of the family line. It should be apparent to the reader at this point that these staves symbolize more than just material goods, though; for one thing, they represent our reputation — Fehu the deeds we achieve in our personal lives, and Othala the fame that is gifted to us with our family name and that we in turn add to with our own accomplishments.

Othala also has connections to other runes. The Othala stave can be seen as a bind-rune of Gebo and Inguz that would mean "the gift of Frey" or "the gift of the garth." As Frey is the lord of peace and fertility, and the garth is the enclosure that defines kin, kith, and property, it would be difficult to find a more appropriate description of what Othala stands for. Frey's gift is offspring — these future generations of family and the folk. These children inherit the garth, then pass it on to their own children when the time comes.

Beyond the material realm of house and land, Othala also encompasses the family name, the luck and reputation of one's kinfolk. When a Viking Age father named and claimed his child on the eighth day after birth, the name he gave his son or daughter was often that of a deceased relative. This was intended to bless the newborn with the luck of the dead kinsman, but it also served as a recognition of the ancestor's spirit that found new life in the child. The Othala gift of the bloodline was thus carried on.

Othala holds close ties to Tiwaz and Ansuz. As the rune of Tyr, Tiwaz represents the maintaining of law, order, and tradition — the pillars of culture. Tyr thus acts as the defender of the heritage that Othala symbolizes. The One-Handed god is conservative in the true sense of the word —

he preserves the old ways so we never forget where we came from. As the rune of Odin, Ansuz represents the winds of change that push us in new directions. The One-Eyed god takes the lead in times of crisis to find a better way forward. The guidance of both these gods has proven necessary time and again for the folk to survive and thrive. Without Tiwaz we are a ship without an anchor, drifting along on the tides with no purpose; without Ansuz we have no sails, destined to be lost and forgotten in the sea of history. The combination of these forces in Othala then can be thought of much like the Roman two-faced deity Janus: one face looking into the past to keep a tight grasp on identity; the other searching into the future with its wary eye for prosperity.

While our ancestors had an immediate physical bond to Othala through blood and soil, today this stave has come to symbolize our heritage as a whole. As such, it embraces a pan-European array of traditions much broader in scope than the local customs any of our ancient forbears would have recognized. This is because many modern Heathens are the descendants of the entirety of Europe. This holds especially true for most Americans, who are separated from their ancestral homelands by hundreds of years and thousands of miles, but even to claim one is English, French, or German belies the fact that these lands have been home to Celts, Romans, Teutons, Scandinavians, and others. To borrow a line from *The Heathen Handbook*, "Knowing your lineage is a wonderful thing, but remember that you are part of a wider ancestral line… the majesty of Greece is ours, the might of Rome is ours, the valor of the Celts is ours, and the fury of the Norsemen is ours."

The shape of the Othala stave itself calls to mind the double helix of our DNA, the coding of which is the collective bloodgift of all our ancestors. Othala thus embodies the essence of what it means to be Heathen: to honor those who came before us, to take pride in our heritage, to live with virtue, and to pass this inheritance on to the next generation.

APPENDIX I - RUNE CASTING

As stated in the chapter on Ancestral Uses, our forebears held omens and auguries to be of great value when making important decisions. Several Roman historians commented on the practice of divination among the barbarians of the North, and many instances have been preserved in both the Eddas and sagas. From these sources we can construct a fairly solid foundation of how traditional rune-casting was performed.

Although entire books are available that focus on various ways of casting and interpreting runes, these methods are often based on those of the Tarot, I Ching, and other systems foreign to our heritage. While other methods are valid and effective within their own traditions, attempts to apply them to the runes are, at the very least, misguided. As we strive to reconnect with the ways of our ancestors, it only makes sense that we come closest to finding them when we tread in their own footsteps. Following other paths can only lead us farther away from our goal.

In working with any form of divination, your ability to discern a meaningful outcome will depend on your knowledge of that system. This holds especially true for the runes, as they are part of the bloodgift handed down to us from our gods and ancestors.

Before attempting a casting, you should be familiar with the mythology and history surrounding the runes, as this will impact the effectiveness of your reading. In *Havamal*, Odin advises us to "know how to carve" and "how to interpret" the staves. (st. 144) At a minimum, you should be able to write down the Elder Futhark in order from memory, along with the names and meanings of each rune.

For those who are new to the runes, memorizing the futhark may seem a daunting task, but with a little effort it can be easily accomplished. Through simple repetition — writing the staves down in order over and over again — you should be able to carve the runes into your mind by dedicating a couple of hours to the task on consecutive days. Once you can identify every rune and its traditional meaning on sight, focus on expanding your understanding of each individual stave by using the information presented in this book and your own sessions of concentration.

Focus on Fehu for a few days until you feel comfortable with it, then spend time with Uruz, Thurisaz, and so forth until you have a grasp of each rune. Although our contemporary culture of convenience has instilled in us an expectation of overnight results, when it comes to learning about the futhark or any other aspect of our heritage, there is no substitute for hard work and perseverance.

Making Your Staves

After you have established a working knowledge of the entire futhark, the next step is to acquire your own set of staves. While there are endless varieties available commercially, our ancestors would have scoffed at the idea of purchasing runes from their version of the local Walmart. A serious runester will take the time to make their own set. Tacitus says the Germanic tribes cut slices from the "branch of a nut-bearing tree," but this may not be practical depending on where you live. Other possible materials include bone or stone, but most Heathens prefer to use some type of wood because of the mythological connection between man and tree. You may have to be creative and use whatever is available to you. In a pinch, we have recycled old Scrabble tiles by sanding off the Roman letters and carving on the runes in their place.

Our ancestors usually colored their staves red. Hilda Ellis Davidson notes that "the runes had to be reddened with sacrificial blood to be effective." It seems that it was the blood of a slain creature that made a sacrifice effective and knowledge of the future possible. For our ancestors, a "sacrifice" did not mean to give something up or destroy it but to make it holy (Heilagr). The ritual shedding of blood would attract the attention of the gods, wights, and Norns alike. While there are instances in the lore of both animals and humans being sacrificed for divinatory purposes, such practices are not part of modern practice.

If you are inclined to color your staves in traditional fashion though, using a small amount of your own blood would be appropriate and potent, especially if the help you seek will be of a personal nature. A good example of this can be found in *Egil's Saga* when the hero carves staves on a poisoned drinking horn, reddens them with his blood, and speaks a charm that shatters the horn and saves his life.

As with the "nut-bearing tree" mentioned above, the use of blood may not be practical or desirable for everyone. If the set of runes you make are intended to be cast in a community setting or will be handled by other people, you might think twice before bleeding on them. For permanent markings such as memorial runestones, our ancestors often used red paint to color their staves, but red ink or marker will work just as well for making a set of runes. It also helps if you have a small cloth or leather bag to store your staves in.

Casting

Rune-casting functions best in a sacred setting. Although some Heathens perform castings during blot, most are done independently of formal ritual. Either way, he act of creating sacred space remains important. For blot, folks often have a special place where they gather to honor our gods and goddesses, and this ground is temporarily set aside for ritual by hallowing it (see *Heathen Handbook*, Sec. VIII). This is usually done by circumambulation (walking in a circle) around the ritual site to establish an imaginary garth.

For rune-casting, the space required is so minimal that walking around it is unnecessary. You may choose to stand in the center of where you will spread out your casting cloth and then face the cardinal directions in turn (N,E,S,W) or you can simply hallow the space in your mind. Different methods work better for different people, but the key is to do whatever you need to do to mentally prepare yourself for the task at hand.

Once you are ready to begin, lay out a white cloth in front of you. If you are using a bed sheet or table cloth, you have the option to cast the runes from a standing position, but keep in mind that the farther the staves have to fall before hitting the cloth the wider they will scatter. Because this makes them much harder to find when it comes to selecting the runes, most people prefer to cast while kneeling down.

Begin by cupping all twenty-four staves in your hands, or, if your runes are too big for this, leave them in their bag and hold it in front of you. Now focus on the question you wish to ask. This is of the utmost importance and needs to be specifically defined. As Carl Jung states, "One must hold in mind the form of the question put, for this sets a definite limit to the interpretation of the answer." You may find it most effective to write down your questions ahead of time. At this point, speak your question out loud, then ask for a blessing. One traditional prayer is, "Thor hallow these runes," but you may prefer "Odin guide my hand," or an appeal to your patron deity or ancestors. Finally, let the runes fall where they may.

Whether or not you were standing while casting, it will be necessary to kneel down to choose your staves. Remember to keep the question foremost in your mind as you begin to feel around for the three runes. It is important that you do not look down at the staves once they have been cast so that you do not "cheat" the process of selection. Either look upwards or keep your eyes closed while choosing.

This may take a few minutes as you feel around for the "right" ones, meaning that your subconscious mind will guide you to certain staves or that they will seem to give off a slight electric current.

Because divination tends toward right-brain functioning, try using your left hand to select the runes and place them in the order they are chosen on your right palm.

Interpretation

The lore offers few clues as to how our ancestors interpreted their castings. At best we can begin with what we know about each rune that has been pulled (the meaning of the rune-name and its significance in our worldview and mythology), then apply what we have learned from our sessions of concentration (projecting the ancient knowledge forward into current times). Even if our ancestors' exact methods remain a mystery, building on the same information they had will at least point us in the right direction.

After you have picked up three runes, take a look at them. Some or all may be face-down, assuming you placed them in your palm just as they were when you lifted them off the cloth. Face-down staves can be related to each rune's negative" aspects, whereas face-up they convey "positive" aspects depending on the interpretation. For a rune such as Kenaz/Kaunaz that means both "torch" and "ulcer," it seems natural to assign the positive aspect to the former and the negative aspect to the latter. Face-up this stave would indicate a guiding light and face-down a period of sickness or suffering.

Of course, few staves have multiple meanings, and we should avoid equating strict value judgments of "good" and "bad" with the positive and negative aspects. For example, Hagalaz means "hail" — a time of crisis. This would be its face-up (positive) interpretation, whereas face-down it would indicate that a crisis had been resolved, "smooth sailing," or at worst, a calm before the storm. In many cases you will have to rely on a combination of knowledge and intuition to determine what a particular aspect indicates within the context of your question.

Some rune books recommend castings that involve selecting any number of staves, but there are a couple of solid reasons that argue for the drawing of three. The most obvious is that the Roman historian Tacitus specifies that the Germanic tribes chose three when casting lots. Again, a core concept of this book is that we come closest to grasping the essence of the runes by adhering to traditional pathways. Since Tacitus provides the most detailed account of divination amongst our ancestors, it only makes sense that we stick to his description.

The other argument in favor of choosing three staves centers around our ancestors' understanding of fate (wyrd). The Eddas speak of three women who sit by the Well of Wyrd at the foot of the World Tree. They are the Norns, the spinners of destiny. Together they weave a tapestry from the threads of wyrd that tells the story of our lives from birth to death. Modern authors usually portray them as metaphors for the past, present, and future, but this oversimplifies their complex interactions.

Urd is the chief and eldest of the Norns, and she can be thought of as representing actions we have already taken that cannot be changed. Verdandi is next, and she symbolizes current events that are being shaped by past actions. Last is Skuld. Her name means "debt," and she represents what is owed based on the deeds that have been and are being performed.

It may be helpful to imagine the Norns as a movie trilogy. Urd would be the first film, one you have already seen but which lays the groundwork for the events of the next two. Verdandi is the second movie, which you are watching right now. Its action builds on what happened in the first movie and would not make sense without it. Finally, Skuld is a sneak preview of the third film, which no one has seen yet. You have some idea of what is going to happen based on where the other two movies were headed, but you are hoping to catch a glimpse of how it all goes down. This glimpse is exactly what we are striving for when rune-casting, and it is likely that our ancestors connected the three staves they drew to the Norns for this same reason.

Examples

Having established our method, the best way to demonstrate how it works in practice is through a series of examples. For these examples we created several fictional scenarios, then drew staves for each. The interpretations that follow are certainly not the only possible ones. They are intended to shed light on the method and all its possibilities.

xample 1

(a) A man in his mid-twenties finds himself unable to commit seriously to a relationship. Even though he wants a family, at the moment of truth, he cannot take the plunge.

(b) A thirty year-old woman is recovering from yet another failed relationship. She gives it her all, but it never seems to work out.

Question (for both) — Why do I keep failing in relationships, and what can I do to change?
Runes (for both) — Tiwaz (face-down), Sowilo, Othala (face-down)
Interpretation :
(a) Urd — Tiwaz (face-down): in this situation, the aspects of Tiwaz that point to sacrifice and selflessness would seem to apply, and the fact that the runestone was face- down indicates a negative aspect, here meaning an absence.

The plunge that the man cannot take involves commitment, which means putting someone else's interests and well-being in front of, or at least equal to, his own. He should concentrate on this rune while looking back at every failed relationship and search for times when his selfishness got in the way of success.

Verdandi — Sowilo: The sun represents the victory of light over darkness and summer over winter. This could point to the man being on the verge of overcoming his difficulties or perhaps being in the ideal time for doing so. Victory also suggests an active struggle, so there should be a lot of focus on how immediate progress can be made that will have a positive impact. If the problem is selfishness, as Tiwaz above would indicate, the man from our example should focus on things he is doing right now that seem selfish and how he can overcome them.

Skuld — Othala (face-down): Othala in the Skuld position is complex because Othala inherently points to the past. Here, because the rune is face-down, Othala seems to indicate a strong possibility that our inheritance — in this case, the things we carry into relationships — can be overcome or negated as we move forward. This should be very encouraging and inspire the man from the example to work hard on getting past his inability to put people he cares about in front of himself.

(b) Urd — Tiwaz (face-down): For a woman, Tiwaz might point to her complement, the male with whom she forms an ideal pair. The stave being face-down in Urd would seem to indicate an absence of that complement and that her past choices in men have not been conducive to success. This is not to say that they were bad men, but that they were not the right men for her. Instead of blaming herself for the failures, she should concentrate on what she sees as the ideal and then question whether that view is realistic or practical. What she has been doing is not working, and this could be the first step in figuring out why.

Verdandi — Sowilo: Sowilo's appearance in this spot is like the sun's appearance at dawn, and it brings to mind the adage: "The first step in solving your problem is admitting you have a problem." The woman's own appraisal of the situation would seem to indicate that she should not be blaming herself for the problem, and recognizing that fact, even embracing it, could be the first thing she does to improve her present. Realizing that her difficulties may stem from bad choices and focusing on how to make better ones will bring her closer to eventual success.

Skuld — Othala (face-down): Othala points toward nheritance, and this inheritance includes ideas about what good relationships look like. Othala face-down may point o possible outcomes that are unconventional or outside the norm, but this break with tradition need not be a bad thing. Perhaps discovering the ideal she was missing will lead her to a place she did not consider possible. If she changes how she approaches relationships and chooses men, the outcome will be very different from what she has previously experienced, and that could be a good thing.

Example 2

A twenty year old man is two years into college and realizes he has no real clue of where he wants his life to go in terms of a profession. He is smart enough and driven enough to do anything but admits his previous plans were unrealistic and is unsure how he should move forward.

Question: Where should I look for a career?

Runes — Uruz, Berkano, Eihwaz

Interpretation :

Urd — Uruz: This rune could be taken two ways. The aurochs points toward power untamed and therefore untapped. The young man's potential has already been mentioned, but thus far it has been unfocused and wasted. Another meaning for this rune is "slag," which is the waste product from smelting ore into usable metal. This could mean that all the effort he has thus far put forward has yielded value for someone (they got the metal) and left him with nothing to show for his work. He should concentrate on this rune and reflect on what led him to pursue goals he now deems unrealistic.

Verdandi — Berkano: This rune could also be taken several ways. Berkano as the sacred feminine, the anima to the young man's masculine potential, could mean that his best path lies outside the ordinary or generally accepted. This could include fields often considered feminine: liberal arts and soft sciences, for example. On the other hand, Berkano could be pointing him toward the path to Asgard, an indication that his potential is truly unlimited if he sets his sights high enough. He should open himself to ideas that are truly unconventional and examine every possibility carefully before he makes a choice.

Skuld — Eihwaz: The Tree that connects all the worlds is an indication of tremendous uncertainty. The decisions he makes now will determine where the path leads — to the edifying success of Asgard, the despondent failure of Niflheim, or anywhere in between. Every road is open.

Example 3

A forty year old woman finds herself divorced, without a professional or financial foundation, and raising two teenagers with almost no help from her ex. She knows she essentially has to start from scratch but is unsure how she should even begin.

Question — What should my immediate goals be, and how can I meet them?

Runes — Dagaz (face-down), Othala (face-down), Raidho

Interpretation :

Urd — Dagaz (face-down): This indicates failure and frustration in moving through the smaller cycles or steps of life, an absence of what should have been incremental growth. The lack of a foundation, and the failure of the marriage, could be the result of the woman's refusal or inability to grow into her situation as life progressed . Because it is unlikely that she can fix her present or future without understanding her past, she needs to concentrate on Dagaz and examine her choices both in terms of her marriage and her growth as a person.

Verdandi — Othala (face-down): This is a lack of the ordinary support and strength of a family. She is doing it on her own, so instead of lamenting the absence of a family's helping hands, she has to figure out how to fill the roles herself. Perhaps the most pressing problem is the lack of the financial support of Othala, and a woman in this predicament cannot refuse to take advantage of whatever options are available to replace that support. No Othala means there is nothing to fall back on, so every decision is critical.

Skuld — Raidho: Moving forward will require focus. The old adage of "One foot in front of the other" may be cliché, but it applies here. She has no option but to get up every day and get the job done, and each time she gets through a day, she will be more confident in her ability to face the next one. Raidho means that her current woes are not the end of the road but the beginning of a new life and new possibilities.

Example 4

A couple is three years from retirement. They have no real health issues and consider themselves financially secure. For the first time in their lives, they can do practically whatever they want. Their problem is that they do not know what they want.

Question — What should we do with the rest of their lives?

Runes — Mannaz, Inguz, Isa

Interpretation :

Urd — Mannaz: Finding Mannaz in this position validates what this couple already appears to know — they have done well for themselves not just financially but emotionally and spiritually as well. Their path to individuation or self-actualization has thus far been successful. To answer their question, they should begin by taking inventory of how they got to this point, make note of their strengths, and use what they find to help guide them into the future.

Verdandi — Inguz: The rune of Frey and the garth points to an internal focus for the present. Rather than looking outside their current lifestyle or location for a positive and fulfilling future, they should look closer to hand. This could mean staying close to family and friends, or it could mean taking something that is already part of their life, like a hobby, and moving it center stage. The garth is not always a physical place. In this instance it could mean a comfort zone.

Skuld — Isa: The ice rune is usually seen as bad or negative, but in this instance, it could point to two possible positive, complementary outcomes. The first is a continuation of past success where the past becomes the present in an unbroken chain. This points to the second outcome, prosperity, where the future path of the couple is unchanging because the stabilizing effect of the ice "freezes" their state of prosperity. This could mean that once they find and embark upon this path, they will follow it for the rest of their days, which is what they are seeking.

Lessons From The Examples

The examples should help illustrate a variety of points. The first is the importance of asking the right question at the outset. The question is the lens through which you will view the casting, and it will therefore color your interpretation. Getting to the proper question sometimes requires self-examination and honesty. If, for example, the man who could not commit to a relationship in the first example had asked, "What is wrong with these women?" he probably would not have learned anything productive.

Casting runes is a means of recognizing patterns in our own unconscious mind, so asking questions that focus on other people is typically an exercise in futility. We go to the runes seeking to better understand ourselves and our situations. Approaching the process with an inadequate or inappropriate question dooms any casting, so choose carefully.

The second point illustrated by the examples is that the runes do not generally present you with definite answers. Instead, they prod you toward asking the right question or at least looking in the right direction for an answer. This is why simple yes/no questions are impractical for rune-casting, and it also why a strong knowledge of the runes and a willingness to honestly examine yourself are so important. Casting the runes usually offers a starting point, a new way to examine a problem or question that has proven unsolvable.

The recently divorced woman from Example 3 faces a mountain of difficulty, and the mountain is so intimidating she does not know whether to climb it, move it, or tunnel through it. The runes do not offer her the secrets of instant success. They do offer a means to begin addressing her problems one by one so she can start rebuilding her life.

The questions any rune leads us to ask should reflect both the order in which it was drawn and the other runes drawn with it. Urd is more than just the past; it is the force of past events as they are active in the present. The question should not just be, "What happened?" but also, "How is what happened still relevant in my life?"

In the same vein, Verdandi is best translated as "Becoming," or how your present is an unfolding of both your past and your personality. The rune in Urd should be a part of the equation in interpreting Verdandi because the reality of the present is always built on the past.

The rune in Skuld should also be considered in the context of the entire casting, because the future is not random or arbitrary. Skuld is the result of all that has come before, so you should determine how the things you learned from interpreting the first two runes can teach you about the third.

The last important lesson we should take from the examples is how intensely personal a successful interpretation must be. In truth, it is nearly impossible to interpret for someone else, and if the interpretations in the examples seem vague or trite, this is a big part of why. Self-knowledge and a willingness to take an honest personal inventory are essential to the process.

The same situation, even the same general question, will point in different directions for different people. Each rune generates a unique interpretation because the wyrd of each of us is unique. Your own wyrd is even subtly different ow than it was a year ago and markedly different from what it was five years ago. Context is everything. This is why the same question and the same runes lent themselves to vastly different interpretations for two different people in Example 1. Interpretation is meaningless without context.

To gain the most from interpreting the runes, take your time and concentrate. A five-minute interpretation will be worth exactly how much time you spent on it. Take a day or a week to concentrate on the rune and ponder how it fits into your wyrd and your question. Hold it up like a gemstone and examine all the ways the light plays off each facet. Interpretation is hard work, and it may force you to acknowledge uncomfortable truths, but putting in the necessary time and effort can yield worthwhile results.

138. I know that I hung
Upon a tree exposed to the wind
Nights all nine, wounded by spear
And given to Odin, myself to myself,
On that tree that no man knows
From where that root runs.

139. Not with a loaf
Or with horn did they bless me,
I looked down, I took up the runes,
Crying out loud, I took them,
Then I fell back from there.

140. Mighty songs nine I learned
From the famous son of Bolthorn, Bestla's father;
And I got a drink of the dear mead
Sprinkled out of Odroerir.

141. Then I learned to make myself fruitful
And to be well-informed,
To grow and thrive as well;
Words from me sought words,
Deeds from me sought deeds.

142. Runes you will find, and counseling staves,
Very potent staves, very strong staves.
That the mighty sage drew
And the great Gods made
And Hroptr carved with power.

143. Odin among Aesir, Dain for elves,

ʃvalin for dwarves, Asvidr for giants,
I carved some myself.

144. Do you know how you should carve?
Do you know how you should interpret?
Do you know how you should draw?
Do you know how you should attempt?
Do you know how you should ask?
Do you know how you should worship?
Do you know how you should send?
Do you know how you should sacrifice?

145. It is better unasked
Than over-sacrificed for,
Always a gift looks for a return;
It is better unsent
Than over-sacrificed for;
Thus Thund carved before the origin of the people
At that place he rose up when he came back.

146. I know that song that prince's wives
And men's sons know not;
Help it is called, and it will help you
With sickness and sorrow
And the whole of affliction.

147. I know another which the sons of men need
Who want to live as healers.

148. I know the third if my need becomes great
For bonds against my enemy,
Blunt I will sing my adversary
So neither his weapons nor guile bites.

149. *I know the fourth if warriors overcome me*
And bind my limbs
I sing so that I am able to walk,
Ungirds the fetter from my foot
And the bonds from my hands.

150. *I know the fifth if I see the shot*
Of a harmful dart rush into the folk,
It flies not with such great force
That I cannot stop it
If I but catch sight of it.

151. *I know the sixth if a thane wounds me*
Upon a strong wooden root,
And that man summons spite against me
Harm will eat him more than me.

152. *I know the seventh*
If I see high flames burning
The hall around my comrades,
It does not burn so brightly
That I cannot save it,
I know that spell to sing.

153. *I know the eighth*
Which to all is useful to learn,
Where hatred grows among the sons of princes,
I can soon heal it.

154. *I know the ninth*
If I stand in need to save my floating ship,
I calm the wind upon the waves
And lull to sleep all the seas.

55. I know the tenth
If I see witches at play in the air,
I work it so that they fare far astray,
From their own skins, from their own minds.

156. I know the eleventh
If I shall lead long-time friends to battle,
Under the shield-rims I sing,
And they fare with power,
Hale to the fight, hale from the fight,
Hale they come hence.

157. I know the twelfth
If I see high upon a tree
A corpse hanging on the gallows,
I carve and draw the runes
Such that the man walks and talks with me.

158. I know the thirteenth
If I should sprinkle water upon a young thane,
He will not fall though into battle he comes
That man will not sink down beneath the swords.

159. I know the fourteenth
If I must tell of the kindred of men
Before the Gods, Aesir and elves,
I remember all knowledge
Few among the universe know such.

160. I know the fifteenth
That Thjodreyrir the dwarf sang
Before Delling's door:
He sang strength to the Aesir,
And luck to the elves,

And knowledge to Hroptatyr.

161. I know the sixteenth if I want to have
All the young maiden's liking and pleasure
I turn the thoughts of the white-armed woman,
And I change all her affections.

162. I know the seventeenth
That the young maiden will not at all avoid me;
These verses will you long lack, Loddfafnir,
Though it would be good if you had them,
Useful if you learned them,
Useful if you accepted them.

163. I know the eighteenth
That I never teach to maid or man's wife,
Anything is better that one alone knows,
Only that one that embraces me as husband
Or is my sister.
This is the end of my verses.

-translated by Thorstein Mayfield

ANGLO-SAXON RUNE POEM

Wealth is a comfort to all men;
 yet must every man bestow it freely,
 if he wish to gain honour in the sight of the Lord.
The aurochs is proud and has great horns;
 it is a very savage beast and fights with its horns;
 a great ranger of the moors, it is a creature of mettle.
The thorn is exceedingly sharp,
 an evil thing for any knight to touch,
 uncommonly severe on all who sit among them.
The mouth is the source of all language,
 a pillar of wisdom and a comfort to wise men,
 a blessing and a joy to every knight.
Riding seems easy to every warrior while he is indoors
 and very courageous to him who traverses the high-
 roads
 on the back of a stout horse.
The torch is known to every living man by its pale, bright
flame;
 it always burns where princes sit within.
Generosity brings credit and honour, which support one's
dignity;
 it furnishes help and subsistence
 to all broken men who are devoid of aught else.
Bliss he enjoys who knows not suffering, sorrow nor
anxiety,
 and has prosperity and happiness and a good enough
 house.
Hail is the whitest of grain;

it is whirled from the vault of heaven
and is tossed about by gusts of wind
and then it melts into water.
Trouble is oppressive to the heart;
yet often it proves a source of help and salvation
to the children of men, to everyone who heeds it
betimes.
Ice is very cold and immeasurably slippery;
it glistens as clear as glass and most like to gems;
it is a floor wrought by the frost, fair to look upon.
Summer is a joy to men, when God, the holy King of
Heaven,
suffers the earth to bring forth shining fruits
for rich and poor alike.
The yew is a tree with rough bark,
hard and fast in the earth, supported by its roots,
a guardian of flame and a joy upon an estate.
Peorth is a source of recreation and amusement to the great,
where warriors sit blithely together in the banqueting-
hall.
The *Eolh*-sedge is mostly to be found in a marsh;
it grows in the water and makes a ghastly wound,
covering with blood every warrior who touches it.
The sun is ever a joy in the hopes of seafarers
when they journey away over the fishes' bath,
until the courser of the deep bears them to land.
Tiw is a guiding star; well does it keep faith with princes;
it is ever on its course over the mists of night and
never fails.
The poplar bears no fruit; yet without seed it brings forth
suckers,
for it is generated from its leaves.
Splendid are its branches and gloriously adorned
its lofty crown which reaches to the skies.

168

ne horse is a joy to princes in the presence of warriors.
    A steed in the pride of its hoofs,
        when rich men on horseback bandy words about it;
        and it is ever a source of comfort to the restless.
The joyous man is dear to his kinsmen;
        yet every man is doomed to fail his fellow,
        since the Lord by his decree will commit the vile
        carrion to the earth.
The ocean seems interminable to men,
        if they venture on the rolling bark
        and the waves of the sea terrify them
        and the courser of the deep heed not its bridle.
Ing was first seen by men among the East-Danes,
        till, followed by his chariot,
        he departed eastwards over the waves.
        So the Heardingas named the hero.
An estate is very dear to every man,
        if he can enjoy there in his house
        whatever is right and proper in constant prosperity.
Day, the glorious light of the Creator, is sent by the Lord;
        it is beloved of men, a source of hope and happiness
        to rich and poor,
        and of service to all.
The oak fattens the flesh of pigs for the children of men.
        Often it traverses the gannet's bath,
        and the ocean proves whether the oak keeps faith
        in honourable fashion.
The ash is exceedingly high and precious to men.
        With its sturdy trunk it offers a stubborn resistance,
        though attacked by many a man.
Yr is a source of joy and honour to every prince and knight;
        it looks well on a horse and is a reliable equipment for
        a journey.
Iar is a river fish and yet it always feeds on land;

it has a fair abode encompassed by water, where it
lives in happiness.
The grave is horrible to every knight,
    when the corpse quickly begins to cool
    and is laid in the bosom of the dark earth.
    Prosperity declines, happiness passes away
    and covenants are broken.

NORWEGIAN RUNE POEM

Wealth is a source of discord among kinsmen;
the wolf lives in the forest.

Dross comes from bad iron;
the reindeer often races over the frozen snow.

Giant causes anguish to women;
misfortune makes few men cheerful.

Estuary is the way of most journeys;
but a scabbard is of swords.

Riding is said to be the worst thing for horses;
Reginn forged the finest sword.

Ulcer is fatal to children;
death makes a corpse pale.

Hail is the coldest of grain;
Christ created the world of old.

Constraint gives scant choice;
a naked man is chilled by the frost.

Ice we call the broad bridge;
the blind man must be led.

Plenty is a boon to men;
I say that Frothi was generous.

Sun is the light of the world;
I bow to the divine decree.

Tyr is a one-handed god;
often has the smith to blow.

Birch has the greenest leaves of any shrub;
Loki was fortunate in his deceit.

Man is an augmentation of the dust;
great is the claw of the hawk.

A waterfall is a river which falls from a mountain-side;
but ornaments are of gold.

Yew is the greenest of trees in winter;
it is wont to crackle when it burns.

ICELANDIC RUNE POEM

Wealth is the source of discord among kinsmen
and fire of the sea
and path of the serpent.

Shower is the lamentation of the clouds
and ruin of the hay-harvest
and abomination of the shepherd.

Giant is the torture of women
and cliff-dweller
and husband of a giantess.

God aged Gautr
and prince of Ásgarðr
and lord of Vallhalla.

Riding is the joy of the horsemen
and speedy journey
and toil of the steed.

Ulcer is disease fatal to children
and painful spot
and abode of mortification.

Hail is the cold grain
and shower of sleet
and sickness of serpents.

Constraint is the grief of the bond-maid
and state of oppression
and toilsome work.

Ice is the bark of rivers
and roof of the wave
and destruction of the doomed.

Plenty is a boon to men
and good summer
and thriving crops.

Sun is the shield of the clouds
and shining ray
and destroyer of ice.

Týr, the god with one hand
and leavings of the wolf
and prince of temples.

Birch is a leafy twig
and little tree
and fresh young shrub.

Man is the delight of man
and augmentation of the earth
and adorner of ships.

Water is an eddying stream
and broad geysir
and land of the fish.

Yew makes the bent bow
and brittle iron
and giant of the arrow.

APPENDIX III - RUNE CHARMS

At the close of the *Runatal*, Odin names his eighteen runes, advising Loddfafnir, "It would be good if you had them." These stanzas should not be mistaken for rune spells themselves, however. Just as the "map is not the territory," so "Help it is called, and it will help you/ with sickness and sorrow and the whole of affliction" is not a rune but a description of its power.

Fortunately, several examples of actual runes can be found in our lore. Although we cannot piece together Odin's entire list of eighteen, a few closely parallel what he describes. By examining them here, we hope to provide the reader with a clearer conception of what the term "rune" meant to our ancestors.

For Healing

I know another which the sons of men need who want to live as healers.

> *Havamal 147*

This spell is obviously one of healing and implies that it covers a wide range thereof. Just such a rune is found in *Lacnunga*, an Old English manuscript (c. 1000 CE) that deals with folk medicine and herbal remedies. This lengthy rune is usually known as the "Nine Herbs Charm" or "Pagan Lay of the Nine Herbs." The following is an excerpt from the charm:

These nine spikes against nine poisons:

A worm came crawling, he tore a man apart,

then Woden took up nine glory-rods,
struck the adder then so it flew apart into nine,
 their apple ended it and its poison
so that it would never bend into a house.
Chervil and fennel, two of great might,
 the wise lord shaped these plants
while he was hanging, holy in the heavens
he set them and sent them into the seven worlds
 for poor and for wealthy, as a cure for all....
Now these nine herbs will avail against nine evil spirits,
 Against nine poisons and against nine infectious diseases,
 Against the red poison, against the running poison,
Against the white poison, against the blue poison,
 Against the yellow poison, against the green poison,
Against the brown poison, against the crimson poison,
 Against snake-blister, against water-blister, ...
Against ice-blister, against poison-blister,
If any poison comes flying from the East or any comes from the
North,
Or any from the West upon the people....

   Mugwort, plantain, which is open eastward, lamb's cress,
cock's spur grass, mayweed, nettle, crab-apple, thyme, and fennel,
old soap; crush the herbs to dust, mix with the soap and with the
apple's juice. Make a paste of water and ashes; take fennel, boil it
in the paste and bathe with egg-mixture, either before or after he
puts on the salve. Sing that charm on each of the herbs; thrice
before he works them together, and on the apple likewise; and sing
that same charm into the man's mouth and into both his ears and
into the wound before he puts on the salve.

   Certainly a rune that countered "nine" diseases (which
is to say, many or all of them) would be of primary
importance to any healer. While this may not be the exact

une Odin refers to in stanza 147, it is likely something very similar. It is also worth noting that it refers to Odin (Woden) "shaping" two of the herbs while hanging from the World Tree, the initiation ritual at the end of which he learns his first runes. ("Mighty songs nine I learned from the famous son of Bolthorn.")

It is also interesting that the charm combines elements of mythology and ritual with the use of medicinal plants. Whether or not the herbs mentioned above would actually work is not as significant as the fact that there are parts of this process that we recognize as "medicinal" in modern terms. The functions of these plants and how to prepare them is just the type of hard-earned knowledge that could be systematized and passed down from one generation to the next.

The somewhat recognizable process of the Nine Herbs Charm can be contrasted with the purely magical ritual preserved in a charm to heal "sudden pain in the sides:"

Feverfew and the red nettle which grows through the house and plantain, boil in butter
Loud were they, lo, when they rode over the hill,
 resolute were they when they rode over the land.
Fend thyself now, that thou mayest survive the violence!
Out, little spear, if herein thou be!
He stood under the targe, beneath a light shield,
Where the mighty women made ready their strength and sent the whizzing spears:
I will send them back another
Flying arrow in their faces.
Out, little spear, if herein it be!
The smith sat, forged his little knife,
Sore smitten with iron,
Out, little spear, if herein thou be!

Six smiths sat, wrought war spears.
Out, spear, not in, spear!
If herein be ought of iron,
Work of witch it shall melt....

Then the direction: "Take then the knife, plunge it into the liquid."

This is an example of what is termed "sympathetic magic," that is, an act done in one place is believed to promote a similar event somewhere else. There is no medicine here, yet it shares with the Nine Herbs Charm the chanting of verses that address the sickness and make mythic references. There was probably a large corpus of such "cures" for diseases which our ancestors did not understand and for which they didn't know a remedy.

Another example of a healing spell has been preserved in the Merseburg Charms, a pair of runes from 8th or 9th century Germany. The second of these speaks of Odin (Wodan) mending the foot of Baldr's horse, but the wording suggests it can be used to counter a "blood sprain" (externally a bleeding wound or internally a sickness) just as well as to heal a broken bone:

To the wood rode Wodan and Balder.
Then sprained was the foot of the filly of Balder.
Then Sinthgund and Sunna her sister sang a charm;
Then Frigga sang a charm, and Folla her sister;
Then Wodan sang a charm, as well he could:
Whether bone-sprain or blood-sprain,
or limb-sprain also:
Bone to bone, blood to blood ,
Limb to limb, as if limed together!

It may be that the second rune of Odin covers all of the spells above. The Nine Herbs Charm would be best utilized as a remedy for poisons and infections, whereas the Merseburg Charm would be more appropriate for binding wounds and setting bones. Spells like the one against sudden pain could have been used where there was no effective tool to fight the sickness, so perhaps they offered a type of placebo-effect. All these skills would be necessary for healers worthy of their reputation, and such individuals likely knew many other spells as well.

For Escaping Fetters

If warriors overcome me and bind my limbs,
I sing so that I am able to walk,
Ungirds the fetter from my foot
and the bonds from my hands.

Havamal 149

Odin's fourth rune appeals to anyone who has ever had the misfortune of wearing restraints. It can be thought of as the Houdini rune — the ability to get out of difficult situations. For an example of such a spell, we look to the first Merseburg Charm:

Once sat the Idisi, sat here and there,
Some bound the bonds, some harried the foe,
Some mixed up the made-fast fetters:
Escape the binding bonds, escape the foe!

Many scholars believe the Idisi mentioned above are the disir, the spirits of one's female ancestors. Here they are pictured as binding and attacking one's enemies while aiding in escape. As the All-Mother, Frigga holds close ties to the cult of the disir, and it may be that these women were seen as goddesses of "loosing" to complement Odin as the god of binding.

Other Runes

The spells we have examined thus far should offer some insight into what constituted a "rune" in ancient times, but it should also be clear by now that the scope of runes goes beyond the spoken word. To cure an illness or free oneself from bondage requires more than an oral entreaty to supernatural forces; physical actions are also necessary. As is often said, "the gods help those who help themselves." Our investigation would thus be incomplete without examples of such actions.

For Counteracting Poisoned Mead

Ale-runes you must know
if you do not want another's wife
to beguile your trust,
if you believe her;
on a horn they should be cut
and on the back of the hand,
and mark your nail with "Nauð."

Sigrdrifumal, 8

This charm can be found in *Sigrdrifumal*, which names a similar but not identical set of skills to those possessed by Odin. This particular rune is intended as a safeguard against poisoned mead, which seems to have been an acceptable means for women to dispose of their male nemies. The valkyrie Sigrdrifa makes sure to teach it to her over Sigurd, as his half-brother Sinfjolti has been killed in precisely this manner.

As with the other runes we have discussed, her description makes it clear that the effectiveness of the spell depends on more than mere word-craft; staves must be carved on the tainted drinking horn as well as on one's hand. As luck would have it, the enacting of just such a rune occurs in the sagas.

Egil Skallagrimsson was an Icelandic poet, warrior, and runemaster. His saga tells how, one night at a blot feast, he suspects the hostess of mixing poison into his drink. He stabs his palm with a knife, carves some staves on his drinking horn, and reddens them with his blood. Only after performing these actions does he speak the following verse:

I carve runes on this horn,
redden the words with my blood,
I choose words for the trees –
of the wild beast's ear-roots;
drink as we wish of this mead
brought by merry servants,
let us find out how we fare
from the ale that Bard blessed.

At the end of his speech, the horn shatters, thus revealing the deadly intent of the mead within. One could argue that simply refusing to drink it would have been just as effective, but doing so would have been a serious breach of etiquette in our ancestors' world. To reject the hospitality of one's host was to violate the code of honor that held society together. On the other hand, attempting to murder guests with poison was apparently fair game.

Although the rune Egil performs here serves the same purpose as that described by Sigrdrifa, there are some differences worth noting. For one, the valkyrie specifies cutting staves on the back of one's hand and fingernail. Egil may well carve Nauð as she suggests, but he does so on his palm. He also takes the additional step of carving staves on the horn.

A more interesting difference is that Egil's spoken verse is not a formula like the Nine Herbs or Merseburg Charms; rather, he composes it on the spot with details particular to the immediate situation. Moreover, he does this on multiple occasions, such as when he heals a girl sickened by "dark letters" (malicious runes) carved on a whalebone. Instead of merely reciting spells that have been passed on to him, Egil demonstrates the ability, like Odin, to create his own runes.

To Stop a Swarm of Bees

From the dire necessity of counter-acting poison, our next rune takes us to the more humble act of farming. Keeping bees was essential to our ancestors both for pollination and honey production. Annual swarming, the sudden departure of much of the hive to a new area, could be devastating.

There were probably many methods used to stop the swarming process, and some were certainly more effective than others. Several charms have survived, including this Anglo-Saxon example that appears free of Christian influence:

Take earth, cast it with thy right hand under thy right foot and say:
I put it under foot; I have found it.

o, the earth can prevail against all creatures, And against injury,
and against forgetfulness, And against the mighty tongue of man.
Cast gravel over them when they swarm and say:
Alight, victorious women, descend to earth!
Never fly to the wood.
Be as mindful of my profit
As every man is for food and fatherland.

Many such charms and remedies survived until modern times. They were passed down as part of the body of knowledge one generation bequeathed to the next. Their efficacy is immaterial to the fact that it was believed that knowing what to do and what to say enabled people to affect their environment.

Curses

If a thane wounds me
upon a strong wooden root,
and that man summons spite against me,
harm will eat him more than me.

Havamal 151

No discussion of ancient charms, spells, or runes would be complete without mentioning curses. Odin says he knows how to counteract a curse carved in runes, so it would seem a safe assumption that he knows how to make one of his own.

People were cursed for vengeance, for spite, and for money in the lore. A few examples can show the variety of curses that might be hurled at an opponent. In the *Second Poem of Helgi Hundingsbana*, Dag breaks his oath to his brother-in-law Helgi and kills him. When Dag tells Helgi's wife Sigrun what has happened, she calls down this curse upon the oath breaker:

May all the oaths which you swore to Helgi rebound on you,
by the bright water of the Leift
and the cool and watery stone of Unn.
May the ship you sail not go forward
though the wind you need has sprung up behind;
May the horse you ride not go forward
though your enemies are about to catch you.
May the sword that you wield never bite for you
unless it's whistling above your own head;
The death of Helgi will be avenged on you
if you were a wolf out in the forest
with nothing of your own and deprived of happiness,
if you had no food
except when you glutted yourself on corpses.

This oath breaker's curse seems to call on things to fail that were either sworn on (touched during the oath) or sworn to (promised to Helgi). The last portion may be a reference to Niflheim, the land of the cursed dead where oath breakers were condemned to suffer. What is notable is that Dag has already done a thing which marks him; all his sister Sigrun does is call down the consequences of his actions.

A different type of curse is found in *Skirnismal* where Skirnir journeys on Frey's behalf to woo the giantess Gerd. When she resists, Skirnir threatens her with terrible repercussions. He says he will strike her with a wand that will banish her to the darkness of Niflheim, turn her into a hideous monster, and torment her with madness and unbearable lust. This is apparently preliminary to the real meat of the curse:

To the grove I went, and to the young forest,
A splendid wand to get, a splendid wand I got.
Angry at you is Odin, angry at you is Thor,
Frey shall hate you, maiden foremost-in-evil,
Not a finger shall the splendidly equipped Gods lift.
Hear me, jotuns! Hear me, frost thurses!
Sons of Suttung, and champions of the Aesir!
How I forbid her the noisy merriment of men,
Deny her the fitness of men.

More terrible threats to the girl, then:

"Thurs" I rist upon you, and three staves –
Perversion and frenzy and anxiety;
Such that I rist on, so may I rist off,
If such becomes fitting.

The curse here is interesting for two reasons. The first is that it threatens to drive the giantess to a state of sexual madness where she is completely unable to restrain herself. It is akin to saying, "I will make you a beast unfit for the company of men." The second interesting element is the combination of invocation and stave-carving that seems to echo that found in *Egil's Saga* and elsewhere.

Another example of a curse occurs in *Egil's Saga* where the hero calls down ruin on the king of Norway and his wife from an island just off the coast:

He took a hazel pole in his hand and went to the edge of a rock facing inland. Then he took a horse's head and put it on the end of the pole. Afterwards he made an invocation, saying, 'Here I set up this scorn-pole [nidstang] and turn its scorn upon King Eirik and Queen Gunnhild' – then he turned the horse's head to face

185

land — *'and I turn its scorn upon the nature spirits that inhabit this land, sending them all astray so that none of them will find its resting place by chance or design until they have driven King Eirik and Gunnhild from this land.' Then he thrust the pole into a cleft in the rock and left it to stand there. He turned the head towards the land and carved the whole invocation in runes on the pole.*

The curse is actually intended to compel the land wights to do Egil's bidding. The curse involves four distinct elements: the sacrifice of the horse, the placing of the pole, the invocation, and the carving of the staves. Incidentally, Eirik and Gunnhild were soon forced to flee Norway.

These curses, like some of the other runes discussed here, are more oriented toward the psychology of the people involved than what we would recognize as some sort of effective process, but the line between magic and method was non-existent among our ancestors. The invocation in a healing charm was just as important as the herbal salve, and the magic words chanted over poison were just as necessary as the poison itself.

SOURCES

Beowulf. trans. R.K. Gordon. Mineola, NY: Dover, 1992.

Chadwick, H.M. *The Cult of Othin*. Cambridge, 1899.

Chaucer, Geoffrey. *Canterbury Tales*. trans. R.M. Lumiansky. NY: Simon and Schuster, 1948.

Davidson, Hilda Ellis. *Myths and Symbols of Pagan Europe*. Syracuse, NY: University of Syracuse Press, 1987.
+*Roles of the Northern Goddess*. London: Routledge, 1998.

Eliade, Mircea. *Shamanism: Archaic Techniques of Ecstasy*. trans. W.R. Task. NYC: Harper and Row, 1961.

Elliott, Ralph. *Runes: An Introduction*. Manchester Univ. Press, 1959.

Faulkes, Anthony and Michael Barnes. *A New Introduction to Old Norse. Vol. II*. London: Viking Society For Northern Research, 1999.

Flowers, Stephen Edred. *Runarmal I*. Smithville, TX: Runa-Raven, 1991.

Geary, Patrick. *Before France and Germany: The Creation and Transformation of the Merovingian World*. NY: Oxford, 1988.

Gimbutas, Marija. *The Goddesses and Gods of Old Europe: Myths and Cult Images*. Berkeley: Univ. of California Press, 1982.

Grigsby, John. *Beowulf and Grendel*. London: Watkins, 2005.

Grimm, Jacob. *Teutonic Mythology*, 4 vols. trans. J. Stallybrass. Mineola, NY: Dover, 1996.

Groenbech, Wilheim. *Culture and Religion of the Teutons*. trans. W.A. Cragie. Oxford, 1933.

Gundarsson, Kveldulf. *Elves, Wights, and Trolls*. Lincoln, NE: iUniverse, 2007

Herbert, Kathleen. *Peace-Weavers and Shield Maidens: Women in Early English Society*. Norfolk, England: Anglo-Saxon Books, 1997.

Holand, Hjalmar. *Norse Discoveries and Explorations in America, 982-1362*. Mineola, NY: Dover, 1969.

Jones, Frederick George. *Old English Rune Poem*. Doctoral dissertation. University of Florida, 1967

Jung, Carl. *The Collected Works of C.G. Jung*. trans. H.C. Roberts. London: Bollinger, 1959.

Mcintosh, Jane. *Handbook to Life in Prehistoric Europe*. NY: Oxford, 2006.

Moynihan, Michael, "Of Wolves and Death." in *Vor Tru 54*. Payson, AZ: World Tree, 1994. p. 14.

Nietzsche, Friedrich. *Basic Writings of Nietzsche*. trans. W. Kaufmann. NY: Modern Library, 2000.

Otto, Walter. *Dionysus: Myth and Cult*. trans. R.B. Palmer. Bloomington: Univ. of Indiana Press, 1948.

Owen, Francis. *The Germanic People: Their Origin, Expansion, and Culture*. NY: Dorset, 1960.

Page, R.I. *Runes*. London: British Museum, 1987.

Poetic Edda: Annotated Heathen Study Edition. trans. Th. Mayfield. Woden's Folk Press. Texas 2020

Pollington, Stephen. *Leechcraft*. Norfolk, England. Anglo-Saxon Books, 2000.

Polome, Edgar C. *Essays Germanic Religion*. Washington, DC: Institute for the Study of Man, 1989.

Porteus, Alexander. *The Forest in Folklore and Mythology*. Mineola, NY: Dover, 2001.

Rydberg, Viktor. *Teutonic Mythology*. trans. R. Anderson. London: Swan Sonnenschein & Co., 1891.

Saga of the Jomsvikings. trans. L. Hollander. Austin: Univ. of Texas Press, 1955.

axo Grammaticus. *The History of the Danes, Books I-IX*. trans. P. Fisher and H.R.E. Davidson. Suffolk: D.S. Brewer, 2006.

Sturlusson, Snorri. *Edda*. trans. A. Faulkes. London: Everyman, 1989.

+*Heimskringla*. trans. A. Smith. Mineola, NY: Dover, 1990.

Tacitus, Cornelius. *Agricola and Germania*. trans. H. Mattingly. London: Penguin, 1948.

Thorsson, Edred. *Futhark: A Handbook of Rune Magic*. York Beach, ME: Weiser, 1984.

+*Runelore*. York Beach, ME: Weiser, 1987.

+*Witchdom of the Tru*. Smithville, TX: Runa-Raven, 2002.

Thorsson, Ornolfr, ed. *The Sagas of Icelanders*. NY: Viking, 2000.

Turville-Petre, E.O.G. *Myth and Religion of the North: The Religion of Ancient Scandinavia*. NY: Holt, Rhinehart, and Winston, 1964.

Watkins, Calvert. *The American Heritage Dictionary of Indo-European Roots*. Boston: Houghton Mifflin, 1984.

Zoega, Geir. *Concise Dictionary of Old Icelandic*. Mineola, NY: Dover, 2004.

About the Authors

Thorstein Mayfield is a founding member of Woden's Folk Kindred and the primary author of *The Heathen Handbook*. He holds a Master's Degree in Comparative Literature from the University of Houston, Clear Lake. For many years he served as the editor of *Heimdall's Horn* and has been a regular contributor to *Vor Tru*. Aside from writing two historical fiction novels, he has successfully fought for the legal rights of Heathens in Texas. He has been active in Heathenry for over 25 years. At the moment, he is in the process of publishing a new translation of the *Poetic Edda*.

Jayson Hawkins holds Master's Degrees in Literature and Humanities with a core in History from the University of Houston, Clear Lake. He is the author of *Blot & Sumbl: A Guide to Heathen Ritual* and a co-author of *The Heathen Handbook*. His articles have appeared in *Ancestral Folkways*, *Heimdall's Horn*, and *Vor Tru*, and he is the editor of *Kvasir*. He has been a part of Woden's Folk Kindred since 2006.

Woden's Folk Kindred is a 501(c)3 church dedicated to reviving the lore and traditions of our ancestors in order to better serve the spiritual needs of people in modern times. We may be contacted at:

wodensfolkkindred.org
Facebook — Woden's Folk Kindred
or write us at

Woden's Folk Kindred
302 Dewberry St.
Waxahachie, TX 75165

Made in the USA
Middletown, DE
02 November 2022

13892956R00120